Microsoft Office for Healthcare Professionals

Microsoft Office for Healthcare Professionals

Beyond Cut, Copy and Paste

Henry I. Balogun, Ph.D.

iUniverse, Inc.

New York Lincoln Shanghai

Microsoft Office for Healthcare Professionals
Beyond Cut, Copy and Paste

Copyright © 2005 by Henry I. Balogun, Ph.D.

iUniverse books may be ordered through booksellers or by contacting:

iUniverse
2021 Pine Lake Road, Suite 100
Lincoln, NE 68512
www.iuniverse.com
1-800-Authors (1-800-288-4677)

ISBN: 0-595-34353-8

Printed in the United States of America

To my mother—Alice Ogunmeowe Omolewa popularly known as "Iya Aladura." You did the best you could for your children with the little you had. You spent your time in obedience to your calling as a servant of God. You did not walk away from those who needed your help. And now you can truly rest in peace. Okun o èye. Suñre ó!

Contents

Acknowledgment

To have four of the most loving, caring and compassionate children in the world is more than a blessing; it is indeed a divine ordination. When they were growing up and I needed the remote control as well as peace and quiet in the living room, all I needed to do was ask "who is doing the dishes tonight?" Every sound of "not me" you hear is usually followed by the closing of the front or the back door. They disappeared faster than you can say "disappear!" Those were the good old days.

Nowadays, it is a different story. TVs are locked on hip-hop stations, CDs of various hip-hop artists are playing at the same time from their bedrooms or the bathroom. When they are not watching music video, it is one boring reality show after another—what a life! Forget about the car radio, I lost my legitimate right to that one a long time ago. Don't even ask me about the home PC; how do you keep more than 10 "Instant Messages" going on at the same time without losing your concentration? I'm telling you, these children (Samuel, Eunice, Joshua and Maryann) makes life worth living. Their energy level along with the joy and fun they bring into my life makes me wish I was 18 again.

Sincere thanks to Dr. Gabriel Bomide for his outstanding review and valuable suggestion.

"Making the simple complicated is commonplace; making the complicated simple, awesomely simple, that's creativity."

Charles Mingus

Introduction to Microsoft Word

Another difficult computer book, huh? No. *Microsoft Office for Healthcare Professionals* is not just a computer book. It is all about providing computer solutions. This is a book for you regardless of your computer background, knowledge or experience. This is not about terabyte, gigabyte, binary code, or high level computer language—you know, the techno-stuff that can send an average person looking for Tylenol for migraine! I don't do stuff like that. You can ask all my friends and they'll tell you I'm the nicest guy in the universe. I'm telling you this is a simple book designed to help you master your *Microsoft Word XP and 2003* as well as your *Microsoft Excel XP and 2003* effortlessly. It is a book for everyone—expert and novice alike.

My primary goal is to provide a high quality, innovative, fun and solutions oriented management tool. My writing philosophy is that the first and the last tasks of a writer and educator are to keep interest alive. This book depicts a real life work environment, thereby making it easier to understand the delicate and technologically packed world of *Word, Graphic and Data* processing. You don't have to be a computer genius to use this book. And anyone desiring to understand the sophisticated world of computer technology should not be labeled "dummy." So, this is not a book for dummy, it is for you the inquiry minds of the world. It is full of graphical interface designed to guide you along the way.

"Not too long ago computers were large, impersonal machines hidden away in glass-enclosed, climate-controlled rooms. To use one, you had to prepare a deck of punched cards and hand them to a professional operator or type cryptic commands, line by line, on a terminal. Today, computers are as accessible and personal as you want them to be." They are less intimidating and continuously opening the door of opportunities to those desiring to understand, in order to become a computer expert, or better yet, Information Technology (IT) professionals.

Within the last decade, word processing and database development software has evolved into a sophisticated, programming oriented and indispensable business tool that can be used by businesses of all sizes. This is a phenomenon that I personally have experienced not only as a student but as a first hand business participant at virtually all levels. If you have not been using a computer, the time to begin is now.

Many people would like to know everything there is to know about the combination of *Word, Graphic and Data* processing now known as Microsoft Office programs but they are too intimidated by overwhelming abbreviations and terminologies. To make this dream a reality for all the daring souls willing to burn the midnight oil in the interest of learning, I've decided to offer a simple but knowledge packed approach, designed to meet the need for varying skill levels. Although, this is written for healthcare professionals, however, it is intended for everyone. Every step and function presented in this book has been tested and proven in most of the Instructor-led classroom training I've offered, geared toward certification in *Microsoft Office User Specialist (MOUS) Program.* Now you can use them in your daily activities. Each chapter is focused and complete. A list of objectives is also provided as a guide to what skills the reader is expected to master in each chapter.

Who should use this book?

If you are concerned about knowing how to use *Microsoft Office—Word & Excel* in a healthcare environment as well as how to use and customize the programs *in Microsoft Office*, this book is for you. If you want to do most of what you thought only the experts can do, this book is for you. If you are concerned about the proper way to handle sensitive information such as patients' record as well as provider information, this book is for you. If you are looking for a book written with the intent to teach you everything you need to become one of the elites in the field of Information Technology without wrapping you in techno jargons and unnecessary terminologies, then, this book is for you. If you are looking for a book that is easy to understand using real life examples, you are looking at it. *Microsoft Office for Healthcare Professionals* is divided into two parts.

Part one covers *Microsoft Word* and part two covers *Microsoft Excel*. Regardless of your prior knowledge and experience, *Microsoft Office for Healthcare Professionals* is written to give you an in-depth knowledge of *Word* and *Excel* and how to better protect sensitive patient information in compliance with HIPAA rules. It covers all the basics including the following (not in the order they are listed below):

1. Mass mailing including all mail merge features.

2. Managing patient and provider information.

3. Document protection focusing on compliance with HIPAA rules.

4. Creating digital certificate to protect sensitive information.

5. Formatting tables in Word and performing calculations in a table.

6. Importing data from other programs.

7. Creating and sending faxes within Microsoft Office.

8. Translate Word document into any language such as Spanish, French, Japanese, Yoruba, Swahili, etc.

9. Creating macros to automate functions that require many steps to accomplish.

10. Step-by-step approach to understanding "IF" function, "LOOKUP" function, "VLOOKUP" function and a lot of difficult to understand formulas in Excel.

11. How to create database.

12. Database management.

13. How to print large database

14. Define or Restrict column(s) in database.

15. Sort and Filter data in a database.

16. Make Excel worksheets part of your website so that visitors to the website can use it to perform any calculations.

17. Integration within Microsoft Office family of programs, and more.

18. General document management.

Notepad

Whenever you see this arrow → always remember that when you perform the action preceding it, the next is the action to which the arrow is pointing. I like to do this to avoid writing long sentences. Isn't that cool! Wait a minute; did you just call me lazy? I'm going to get you for this—no doubt.

This book assumes you are no stranger to Windows Applications. It also assumes you are well skilled in typing. Although this is not a book about typing, using

Word Processing involves typing most of the time. Try as much as possible to improve your typing skills.

Notepad

Do not rush through the steps in this book. If you mistakenly click a choice different from what is suggested, don't panic. Take time to read whatever pops up and gracefully get out of it before you do anything else. Not only that, always make sure to finish each step before moving to the next. You are not trying to run faster than the man in front. In this case, you are the man in front. Don't try to outrun yourself. Just follow each step carefully. Good luck!

Microsoft, Microsoft Excel, Microsoft Word and *Microsoft PowerPoint* are the copyrighted trade marks of Microsoft Corporation.

> "Choice, not chance, determines one's destiny."
>
> Unknown

Chapter One

Optional Configuration— Fine-tuning Your Computer System

Objectives

When you finish this chapter, you will be able to:

- Change the icons on a desktop from using double click to a single click
- Change the start menu base on your preference
- Work from the same window and avoid cluttering up your computer screen with so many windows.
- Add a little more speed to your computer
- Handle accessibility features
- Handle StickyKeys with or without the mouse

Microsoft Office for Healthcare Professionals is designed to bring you into the beautiful world of automation, integration and animation while addressing functions of management. But before we begin, we are going to make some minor adjustment (remember, this is optional) to simplify movement within the system.

First of all, you may want to change the icons on your desktop from using double click to a single click everywhere. If that is the case, let's perform these simple steps together.

Steps

1. Click **Start** and then move your mouse to **Programs** from the list of programs in your system, look for and click on **Windows Explorer**. (If you are using Windows XP, click the **Start** button, put the mouse on **All Programs** and then click **My Computer**.)

2. Click **Tools** → **Folder Options** (for those using Windows 98, ME and 2000, click **Settings**). That should take you to a screen that looks like the following:

3. Click the **General** tab, in the **Click items as follows** section, click on the radio button labeled **Single-click to open an item (point to select)**

4. Click **Ok**.

From now on, all you will need to access any icon (on your desktop and virtually everywhere) is a single-click and not double-click anymore.

Do you know that you can change the new *Windows XP* start menu? If you don't like the default start menu, you can change it to the *Classic Start* menu you are used to, thereby making it look like your *Windows 95, 98, ME* and even *2000* start menu.

To change your Start menu

1. **Right Click** on the **Start** button **Start** or anywhere on the **Taskbar**

2. Click **Properties**

3. When the *Taskbar and Start Menu Properties* window pops up, click the **Start Menu** tab and then click the radio button next to **Classic Start menu**

4. Click **Ok**

Work from the same window

If you are like me, a nice guy who prefers to have any new item in my computer open in the same window, you are going to like this one. As for me, I get frustrated with the clutter created by a new window opening separately, most especially, when I'm using Windows Explorer. Yeah, what about my desk! Don't even go there. I like it the way it is. I'm talking about cluttering up your computer screen with so many windows. Do you know you can solve this problem easily! Let me show you how.

Windows 98

1. In My Computer or Windows Explorer, Choose **View → Folder Options.**

2. Click to activate the **General** tab (if not already activated) on the *Folder Options* window.

3. Click the radio button next to **Custom, based on settings you choose,** and then click **Settings.**

4. From the *Custom Settings* window, click **Open each folder in the same window.**

5. Click **Ok.**

Windows XP

1. In My Computer, choose **Tools → Folder Options.**

2. Click to activate the **General** tab (if not already activated) on the *Folder Options* window.

3. Click the radio button next to **Open each folder in the same window.**

4. Click **Ok.**

Add a little more speed to your system

Windows 98

1. Click **Start → Programs → Accessories** and from the **System Tools**, click **Disk Defragmenter.** This should take you to a small pop up window.

2. Click **Settings** and on the Disk Defragmenter Settings, click to place a check mark in the check box next to **Rearrange program files so my programs start faster.**

3. Click **Ok.**

Windows XP

1. Click **Start → All Programs → Accessories** and from the **System Tools,** click **Disk Defragmenter.** This should take you to a small pop up window.

2. On the Disk Defragmenter window, click one of the following:

   a. Analyze

   b. Defragment

3. When you have finished, simply close the window

Dealing with Accessibility Features

For some strange reasons, I get unsolicited e-mails everyday, and some of them are downright rude and annoying. I'm the type of person who would not mind to delete e-mails from an unrecognized source without reading them, but when I got to this one, something prompted me to read and this is what it says:

I was at my bank to make a deposit when the clerk behind the counter turned to the computer for information. As she touched a button, a small part suddenly flew off the machine. All sorts of odd symbols started flashing across the screen. I heard her gasp, and then she turned to me in wide-eyed wonder and exclaimed, "It's swearing at me!"

I'm quite sure that this was designed to amuse its readers, but when you really look at the way most computer users handle accessibility features, don't be surprised if you sat down at your friend's computer and the system is swearing at you. How is that possible? Let's assume you inadvertently left the microphone on, and someone is really upset in the other room and yelling some inappropriate vocabularies. Believe it or not, if the microphone is turned on, and the system is in dictation mode, don't be surprised if the computer system starts displaying what the irate host is saying, word for word.

Useful Windows Shortcuts to handle accessibility features

1. To turn the microphone on or off, hold down the **Windows logo** key and press **V**.

2. To turn the handwriting feature on or off, hold down the **Windows logo** key and press **H.**

3. To switch between voice command mode and dictation mode, hold down the **Windows logo** key and press **T.**

StickyKeys

In case you have a friend, a family member, a co-worker or just an acquaintance who is having a difficult time holding down two or more keys at a time, StickyKeys is the answer. When a shortcut requires a key combination, such as **Ctrl + Alt + Del** or **Ctrl + B** for bold, or **Ctrl + P** for print, or **Ctrl + Esc** to activate Windows start menu (good for keyboards without Window logo), StickyKeys will make it possible for you to press one key at a time instead of pressing them simultaneously as is programmatically required. Always remember that the Stickykeys is there if you want to use the **Shift, Ctrl,** or **Alt** key by pressing one key at a time.

All right, no doubt about the usefulness of the **StickyKeys** but where in the universe is the **StickyKeys**! One thing you really don't want to do is try to look for it without knowing where to find it. It is not part of the keyboard keys or in a combination of keys. You simply need to call it into existence just by turning on its shortcut feature or by using the mouse to hunt for it. Let's use its shortcut feature to turn it on when we need it, or off when we don't have to use it.

To turn it on, press the **Shift** key on your keyboard **five times** and that will bring out the following popup window: (If your system does not respond to this simple command, follow the instruction on the next page.)

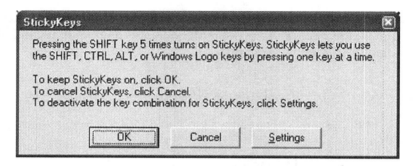

Although information on the *StickyKeys* window is self-explanatory, there is more to it. If all you want to do is simply turn on the *StickyKeys*, you can just go ahead and click **Ok,** otherwise, click **Settings** for more choices. For now let us click **Ok.** To experience the beauty of the *Stickykeys*, press this keys (**Ctrl + Esc,** or **Ctrl + Alt + Del** [be careful not to inadvertently turn off your computer system prematurely], or try any **Shift, Ctrl,** or **Alt**) one key at a time.

To turn on StickyKeys using the mouse

1. Click the Windows **Start** button

2. Click **Setting** → **Control Panel.** If you are using Windows XP, click **Start → Control Panel**

3. Double click the **Accessibility Options** icon and that should bring out the following window:

4. Click the box next to **Use StickyKeys**.

5. In addition to turning on the *Stickykeys* from the *Accessibility Options*, you can also turn on the **ToggleKeys** to add tones each time you press the **Caps Lock,** or **Num Lock,** or **Scroll Lock.** This is really neat especially when the reading glasses are not as good as they ought to be. When you hear the tone(s), you know for sure that the Cap Lock or the Num Lock or the Scroll Lock is on. But if the reading glasses are still as effective as ever or the contact lens hasn't fallen off, you might not want to be bothered with the *ToggleKeys*.

6. Click **Ok**.

Notepad

If the activation of the *StickyKeys* or the *ToggleKeys* result in conflict with the system, it is advisable to turn it off immediately and use it only when you need it.

Chapter Two

What is Microsoft Office?

Objectives

When you finish this chapter, you will be able to:

- Identify the component programs of *Microsoft Office*
- Get started with Microsoft Word
- Recognize and use the Access Keys
- Use the AutoCorrect feature
- Show shortcut keys in Screen Tips
- Show all menu commands in Microsoft Office

Microsoft Office is a family of computer programs bundled up into one. They call it (Microsoft) Office not because it is meant for use in an office environment only even though most of the programs in Microsoft Office are geared toward office users. However, Microsoft Office (consist of *Word, Excel, PowerPoint, Outlook, Access* and in most cases *FrontPage*) is for you regardless of what you intend to use it for—personal use or business use. *Microsoft Office for Healthcare Professionals* is designed to help you in your quest to fully understand these three programs:

1. *Microsoft Word.* This is a program designed to assist you in virtually every aspect of document creation. If you are a constant user of word processing software, get on the band wagon of the most widely used word processing program on the planet.

2. *Microsoft Excel.* This is a program popularly known as an electronic spreadsheet designed to make working with numbers (regardless of whether you are actually comfortable working with numbers or not) something to really enjoy and not something to despise. There is simply no better electronic spreadsheet or worksheet as some people like to refer to it.

3. *PowerPoint.* There is no program capable of enabling any professional to create multimedia presentations like *PowerPoint.* However, one thing *PowerPoint* doesn't do, contrary to public opinion, is create presenta-tions—people do. PowerPoint is a tool. You can use this powerful program to create visual aids necessary for giving an exquisite presenta-tion. I am going to show you how you can create stunning PowerPoint slides, pictures, sounds, video clips, music, animations, charts and a host of other elements.

These programs' graphical user interface makes them so easy that even a first time user will start doing meaningful things right from day one. What about integra-tion within the rest of Office programs as well as web integration? Just what the doctor ordered. Their powerful charting and formatting features make displaying your data (any way you so desire) something to talk about. Go ahead and turn on your computer system and let us explore the wonderful world of *Microsoft Word, Excel and PowerPoint.* Oh, one more thing. We are going beyond just cut, copy and paste. In that regard, I expect you to have a minimum knowledge of how to use the mouse—that's all the preliminary knowledge you are expected to have. Is that too much to expect? If you don't, I strongly advise you take "Mouse Click 101." Don't ask me who is offering it and where, I have no idea.

To Start Word

• From the desktop, click on **Start** button usually located at the bottom left corner of your desktop.

• Place your mouse on **Programs**, or **All Programs** (if your system is equipped with Windows XP) from the right pane, look for and select **Microsoft Word.**

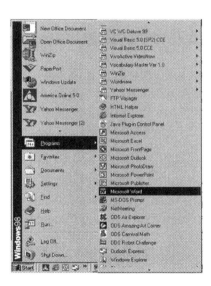

• Microsoft Word will open and the title bar will say "Microsoft Word— Document 1" In case a "Tip of the Day" appears on your screen when you open Word, you must click on **Ok** after reading it, to close the dialog window.

If you already have your **Microsoft Office shortcut bar** loaded on your desktop, click ▣ button on the **shortcut bar** to open **Word**. Opening your Microsoft Word should take you to a screen similar to the following:

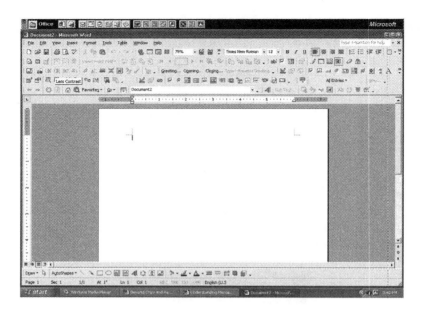

If your screen doesn't look exactly like mine, don't worry. I usually have a lot of tool-bars open for quick and easy access. I'm not trying to show off my beautiful screen shot, am I? I just want to let you know that here is where you do all your creating, editing, formatting, automation, integration and animation of document(s).

The Access Keys

Let us look carefully at the menu choices available in your Microsoft Word and you will discover that some letters are underlined and some are not.

File Edit View Insert Format Tools Table Window Help

The underlined letters are called **Access Keys**. Let's assume that something happened and you are freaking out because you think Freddie Kruger is in the room, and let's also assume that in the process of trying to kill Freddie you mistakenly step over your mouse and break it into little pieces, don't worry about the mouse. All you need to do is hold down the **Alt** key and press F. This will take you to where you can E**x**it gracefully—no, not from the room but from your Microsoft Word. After that, you can easily turn around and deal with Freddie in your own way.

Each underlined letter works with the **Alt** key. Hold down the **Alt** key and then press any of the **Access Keys** (the underlined letter) and it will activate the pull down menu. On the pull down menu, you will discover that some letters are also underlined; you can just press any of those without using the **Alt** key. For example: to open a file without using the mouse

1. Hold down the **Alt** key and press **F**

2. On the pull down menu, press **O** and that will activate the **Open** dialog window.

3. From the **Open** dialog window you will have to use the **Alt** key again along with any of the **Access Keys** showing in your **Open** dialog window to access the area of interest to you.

This does not mean that you should just go ahead and get rid of your mouse, ok? We all like the point and click, don't we?

Minor Configurations in Word

For the sake of the project we are about to do together, we are going to make some minor adjustment to your system. The first will involve making sure the system knows your name, initial and address so we would not have to input them every time we need them. The second will be to inform the system about some common abbreviations we are going to be using. After that, we are going to require every toolbar button to display shortcuts as well. The last minor configuration necessary for our project will have to do with the way Microsoft Office displays menu options once we click on it or activate it using any of the access keys.

Let's go ahead and put your name, initial and address in the system if you don't already have them there.

Steps

1. On **Tools**, click **Options** and you should see a screen exactly like the following:

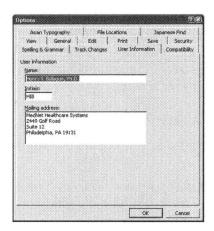

2. Click the **User Information** tab to enter your <u>Name</u>, followed by <u>Initials</u> and <u>Mailing Address.</u>

The next one is **AutoCorrect.**

One of many features of *Microsoft Office* you are really going to appreciate is AutoCorrect. With AutoCorrect you can type a word or abbreviation and Word will replace it with the exact text you specified in the AutoCorrect dialog window. This is a feature perfect for legal, medical, or any other specialized environment. Type an abbreviation, and AutoCorrect will convert it to the correct word or phrase.

When you type a word already specified in the list incorrectly, it will automatically be corrected. By default, the AutoCorrect feature already includes many commonly misspelled words. Needless to say, you can go ahead and add your own problem words to the AutoCorrect list. That is exactly what we are going to do right now.

Steps

1. To create a new AutoCorrect entry, choose <u>**T**ools</u> → <u>**A**utoCorrect</u>.

2. Type the misspelled word or abbreviation in the **Replace text box**. For the sake of our project here let us type <u>ADHD.</u>

3. Type the correct word or phrase in the **With text box**. Let's type <u>Attention Deficit Hyperactivity Disorder,</u>

4. Click the **Add** button to add more to the list. Add the following primary diagnosis:

Replace	With
ODD	Oppositional Defiant Disorder
PDD	Pervasive Developmental Disorder
DBD	Disruptive Behavior Disorder NOS
AISD	Alcohol-Induced Sleep Disorder
OCD	Obsessive Compulsive Disorder
PTSD	Posttraumatic Stress Disorder

5. Click **OK** when you are finished adding entries.

Notepad

To test the **AutoCorrect** on your blank screen, type any of the abbreviations and press the **Enter** key or even the **space bar** and the system should replace the abbreviation with the full name. However, if you want to prevent all automatic corrections, choose **Tools** → **AutoCorrect** and clear the **Replace Text as You Type** check box.

Show Shortcut Keys in ScreenTips

What is Screen Tips? To put it simply, screen tips tells you what an icon or a button is all about and if anything, what it is supposed to do. Move your mouse over to any of the toolbar buttons now displayed on your screen and you will see either a name or description of the button. To help you master some of the shortcuts available in your Microsoft Office, we are going to configure those buttons to show shortcut keys along with the name or description of each button. Please bear in mind that this feature works perfectly well in all of Microsoft Office applications except Excel. To display shortcut keys in ScreenTips:

Steps

1. On the **Tools** menu, click **Customize**, and then click the **Options** tab.

2. If it's not already selected, select the **Show ScreenTips on toolbars** check box.

3. Select the **Show shortcut keys in ScreenTips** check box.

Show All Menu Commands in Microsoft Office

Microsoft Office XP and *Office 2003* are both designed to display only the commands that you use most often each time you click any of the menu options. However, if you want to see all of the commands displayed the moment you click any of the menu options just like in Office 97 and Office 2000, you would have to make a minor adjustment. This adjustment is necessary to avoid confusion and a statement such as: "I can't find the choice the book is asking me to click." For this adjustment, we are going to ask the system to display menu choices on click. To turn off personalized menus:

1. On the **Tools** menu, click **Customize**, and then click the **Options** tab.

2. To show all the commands on the menus, clear the **Menus show recently used commands first** check box. (In Microsoft Office XP, you will click the check box that says **Always show full menus.**)

Can you believe that once you've done it in one of *Microsoft Office 2000 or XP* program's you've done it in all! Yep, I'm telling you, you are becoming a force to be reckoned with. There are some other configurations we could have made but for now we are just going to move right along into the main reason the book has been written.

"If you think education is expensive, try ignorance."

Derek Bok

Chapter Three

Business Letter

Objectives

When you finish this chapter, you will be able to:

- Create company letterhead using the Page Setup
- Create company letterhead using Header and Footer approach
- Create a directory
- Open an existing document
- Save all your files at once
- Open more than one file at once

Let me introduce you to Ms. Jones. She is the Clinical Director of MidMed, a very large Outpatient Psychiatry right here in this beloved city of ours. Not long ago, she requested to have a separate *Microsoft Office* installed in her Secretary's computer system. This is in addition to having access to the one already installed in the company's Network Server. Our job is to assist Ms. Jones' Secretary to get more done in less time. She is going to be overwhelmed unless we lend a helping hand. Notwithstanding, the time to get more organized in order to become much more effective and efficient is now.

Ms. Jones would like to find a way to automate her clinic functions. She is under pressure from management to cut cost and increase productivity. Her first strategy is to create documentation on demand. According to her, this would lead to elimination of wasteful spending. She is meeting with the Medical Director as well as other staff members next week to discuss centralization of Intake, Scheduling, Medical Record and Assignment of Patient per Clinician.

The first assignment is to find a way to eliminate patient no-shows, thereby reducing idle time on the part of both Psychiatrists and Therapists. To accomplish this productivity driven objective, we are going to help her Secretary to develop a letter that she can use to remind every patient (on demand) not to forget about previously scheduled appointments with Psychiatrists and Therapists in the clinic. We are determined to help her Secretary develop whatever other documentations are required. We've got to do a good job because Ms. Jones is a consummate professional who will not settle for anything less than the best.

Assumptions

- We are going to assume that the clinic does not have a standard letterhead for this type of correspondence. In that wise, we are going to create one right now for the letter we are about to develop for the clinic.

- We are also going to assume that there is no existing data source (database) to pull from and in that case, we are going to create a data source to accommodate all the 1500 patients of the clinic. What? C'mon, this is really nothing to sneeze about. The front desk person is very good and genuinely believes in team work. She is going to help us input information into our data source as soon as it is created. In this case, your job is just to create and the front desk people will do the rest. Is that fair enough?

Creating Company Letterhead using Page Setup

To create a professionally looking letter head using page setup approach, let us follow this simple step-by-step approach. It is not advisable to skip any of the steps or assume you know it before attempting it. Let us do it together.

Steps

1. Choose **File** → **Page Setup**. Set the top margin to 0.5"

2. Click **Ok.**

3. Click **Format** → **Font** and that should give you a screen like the following:

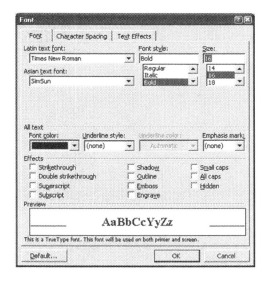

4. Under **Font style**, choose **Bold**. Under **Size**, choose **16** and under **Font color**, choose **Dark Red**.

5. Click **Ok.**

6. Type **MidMed** and press **Enter**.

7. Click **Align Right** or simply use the shortcut which is **Ctrl + R**

8. Repeat step 3 above but don't forget to change the **Size** to **11** and under **Font color**, choose **Dark Blue**.

9. Click **Ok.**

10. Type the following exactly as written below—single spaced.

> **2359 Lakewood Road,**
> **Philadelphia, PA 19142**
> **Phone (215) 555-1212**
> **Fax (215) 555-6767**

11. Click **Align Left** or **Ctrl + L** to move the cursor (not the address you just typed) back to the left.

When you finish, your screen should look similar to the following:

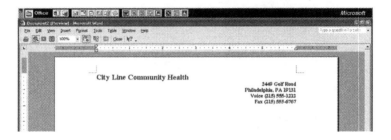

Create company letterhead using header and footer approach

1. Open a blank page. Click **View → Print Layout** if the page is not already in print layout.

2. Click **View** again and choose **Header and Footer.**

3. While header and footer is displayed, click **Format → Tabs**, on the following screen,

4. Click **Clear All**, and then click **OK**.

Clearing the default tabs set for the header and footer allows you to insert your letterhead information at any .5" interval.

5. On the **Formatting** toolbar, choose the font type, font size, and font color to reflect the previous selection.

6. Type the company name, press the TAB key on your keyboard six times, and then type the company telephone number.

7. Type the company street number and name.

8. **Note** If you have a short street address, you may need to press TAB seven times rather than six until your insertion point is aligned with the telephone number above, and then type the company fax number.

9. Press ENTER, and then type the company city, state, and ZIP code.

10. Press the TAB key again until your insertion point is aligned with the fax number above, and then type the company e-mail address.

11. On the **Header and Footer** toolbar, click **Close**.

Insert company letterhead on page one only (recommended)

When you finish typing your letter and the letter is longer than one page, if you do not want company letterhead to appear on each page, complete the following steps.

1. Choose **File** → **Page Setup**.

2. On the **Layout** tab, under **Headers and footers**, select the **Different first page** check box.

Insert company mission statement or special message in the footer

1. Assuming you are still in Print Layout, click **View** → **Header and Footer**.

2. On the **Header and Footer** toolbar, click the **Switch Between Header and Footer** button.

3. On the **Formatting** toolbar, choose the font type, font size, font color, and alignment option you want.

4. Enter the company message, or mission statement

5. If your letter is longer than one page and you want the footer information to appear on each page, on the **Header and Footer** toolbar, click the **Show Next** button, and then enter the company message, mission statement, or logo.

6. On the **Header and Footer** toolbar, click **Close**.

Let us save this portion as a template. In that wise, we can always come back to use it again and again. But before we do, Let us not forget that this is a project and the letterhead we just created is the first among many documents including data source (database) we are going to create for this project. One thing we would like to do is keep our project well organized.

Organizing a project

Our number one goal is to create a project folder (directory). This would make it easier for us to locate any file created as part of this project. I am going to urge you not to rush but follow these steps very carefully.

12. Click the **Save** button or simply go to **File** → **Save** and the following screen pops up.

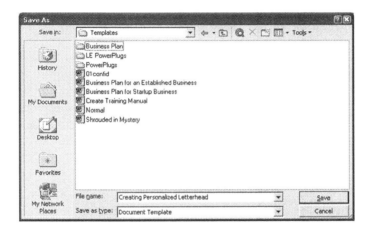

13. Click the arrow next to the **Save in** box and select **Local Disk (C:)**. What this means is that your new directory is going to be placed in the root directory of your C Drive.

14. After that, move your mouse (don't click) on the second manila folder to the right of the **Save in** box and it should read **Create New Folder**. Click on it and you should see the following screen:

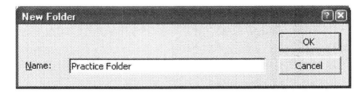

15. In the **Name** box, type "**Practice Folder**" as the name of your new directory or folder.

16. Click **Ok**.

17. Type a name for your letter head in the **File name** box.

18. In **Save as Type**, click **the arrow** next to the box and choose **Document Template**.

19. It is very likely that the name showing in the **Save in** box has changed to "Template." Kindly make sure you are paying close attention. If that is the case, click on the box itself, choose **Local Disk (C:)** and you should see a directory named "Practice Folder" (the directory you created in steps 12 through to 16). Click the directory, and then

20. Click **Save**.

Exiting Word

After using Word or any of the programs or applications in Microsoft Office (or any other program for that matter), you should always make the effort to exit the application gracefully. Microsoft Word is designed to perform necessary house-keeping before it closes.

If after you click save you decided to modify your document and let's assume that changes to the document have not been saved, any attempt to exit will compel Word to bring out a small pop up window asking the following question:

Do you want to save the changes to "File Name"

All you need to do is click **Yes** for Word to save changes to your document before leaving the program.

Saving All Your Files at Once

In case you have more than one document open in Word, you can save them all at once or close them all at once. Anything that can help improve productivity is excellent in a busy office environment. Let us unfold some of the hidden secrets and helpful hints of Microsoft Word.

1. Hold down the **Shift** key and click **File** menu. When you hold down **Shift**, two new options appear on the **File** menu that wouldn't appear ordinarily: **Close All** and **Save All**.

2. If you have more than one document open and you want to save them all, click **Save All**.

3. To close all your open documents, click **Close All**; In this case, Word will prompt you to save your changes before closing any documents.

To exit *Word* gracefully, choose **File** followed by **Exit**. For the sake of our project, let us exit *Word* right now.

Opening an Existing Document

There are several ways you can open an existing document. One way is to go straight from your desktop to the document you were working on last. Your Windows operating system is designed to remember some of your most recent files making it easier to open any of those files. Another way is to open Word and then open any of your existing documents. Let us try opening our last document from the desktop.

From Windows XP

Click **Start** and place your mouse on **My Recent Documents**. There you will see the list of your most recent documents. Click on the one you want to open and that should activate and open *Microsoft Word* along with the document.

From Windows 95, 98, ME and 2000

Click **Start** and place your mouse on **Documents**. There you will see the list of your most recent documents. Click on the one you want to open and that should activate and open *Microsoft Word* along with the document.

From inside Word

1. Choose **File → Open** or click the **Open** button on the Standard toolbar, or simply hold down the **Ctrl** key and press **O**. Either way should take you to the following window:

2. Click on the **Look In** box to select the drive followed by the folder where the document you want to open is located and the contents of the folder should appear. In our case, let us open our last document—the Letter Head Template.

3. Once the file is located, click on it once and click **Open.**

Open more than one file at once

4. To open more than one file at the same time, click **on the first file**, hold down the **Ctrl** key while you click **on the second file** and **the third** and so forth Once all the files you want to open are highlighted, click **Open.**

Before going to the next chapter, kindly make sure the letterhead you created earlier is now open and active on your screen.

> "A great pleasure in life is doing what people say you cannot do."
>
> Walter Gagehot

Chapter Four

Working with Document

Objectives

When you finish this chapter, you will be able to:

- Create Mail Merge document
- Create Database for Mail Merge using Microsoft Word
- Insert Merge Fields to your document

We are going to type the following letter exactly as it is into the template we have created, saved and now opened. We are going to use single space within paragraph and double space between paragraphs. We are going to type it with all the mistakes, extra spaces in paragraph one, and with all the spelling errors just exactly as they are (please do not make corrections while you are typing). As for the special characters such as © and ½ do not worry about trying to insert those right now. You will have the chance to insert them later on.

In a standard business letter, information is typically left-justified (along the left margin) and flows down the page in the following order:

1. Current date

2. Recipient's name and address

3. Salutation (opening greeting)

4. Body of the letter, containing the text or message of the letter

5. Complimentary closing followed by a comma. Example of acceptable complimentary closing is "Sincerely"

6. Signature block (name on one line followed by the title on the next line). There are usually four spaces between "Sincerely" and the signature block

7. Reference initial—this usually contains the initial of the typist in lower-case

8. Enclosure notification follows

9. Copy notation is usually the last line. Example: c: Henry I. Balogun, Ph.D.

MidMed©

2449 Golf Road
Philadelphia, PA 19131
Voice (215) 555-1212
Fax (215) 555-6767

February 17, 2005

Dear

This is to remind you of your previously schduled appointment with   for Medication check on Thursday, January 29, 2003 at 10:30 am, and also with   for psychotherapy at 11:00 am. You are hereby adviced to arrive early. Your total time at the clinic is expected to be 1½ hours.

If you have any questions or concerns, or you are going to be late for whatever reasons, feel free to call me at (215) 999-6161 or call your Psychiatrist and Therapist directly. Their numbers are as following:

When coming, kindly remember to bring the follownng with you:

Insurance card
Social Security card; and
Photo identification

Sincerely,

Maria Villanueva
Secretary

cm
Enclosure
c: Front Desk Personnel

Mass Mailing

There is currently no data source that contains the list of names and addresses for the patients at the clinic where Ms. Jones works. We are going to create one using the *Mail Merge Wizard*. This is not the only way we can create the data source. You can also use address information from *Outlook and Schedule+* or *Microsoft Excel spreadsheet* or *Access database*. Also, there are some third party applications such as Medical Billing or Practice Management software that will let you integrate with its database using Microsoft Word or Excel. Regardless of how your data source (database) is created, you simply need one!

Create Database for Mail Merge using Microsoft Word

A main document could be a letter, an envelope, agreement or other document that you would like to send to a lot of people or perhaps one person at a time through the convenience of mail merge. They usually contain codes that will be replaced with entries from a data source of names and addresses. The main document has the Mail Merge task buttons on the Mail Merge toolbar, which is the launching point for the other Mail Merge tasks. When creating a main document for a mail merge, you can use an existing document or create a new document. In either case, you need to define the document as the main document for the mail merge. In our case, we are going to use the document we created earlier.

Notepad

The Mail Merge Task Pane interface shown here is taken from *Microsoft Office 2003*. If you are using *Word 97* or *2000* please visit www.mednetservices.com to download Mail Merge instructions.

Steps

1. Open the existing document.

2. Choose **Tools** → **Letters and Mailings** → **Mail Merge Wizard** to display the Mail Merge Task Pane. The task pane displayed on the right side of your screen should look exactly like this:

The **Mail Merge** task pane "*Step 1 of 6*" opens with a question about what type of merged document you are creating. If you have fax support set up on your computer and a fax modem installed, you will also see **Faxes** on the list of document types—for instruction on setting up Windows Fax utility turn to chapter six (Internet Integration and Sending Fax).

3. Click the radio button on Letters to select **Letters**.

4. Click **Next: Starting document** at the bottom of the task pane. And that should take you to the following screen which is *Step 2 of 6*:

5. Click to select the radio button next to **Use the current document**

6. Click **Next: Select recipients** at the bottom of the task pane and that should lead you to the following screen:

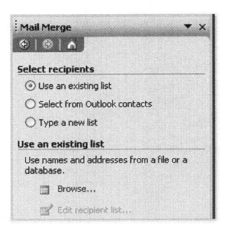

7. We do not have an existing data list, in that wise, we are going to create a new data list. Click **Type a new list** → **Next: Write your letter**, and then use the form that opens to create your list. The list is saved as a mailing database (.mdb) file that you can reuse.

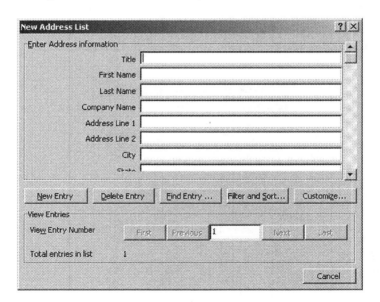

8. Click **Customize** to get the next screen.

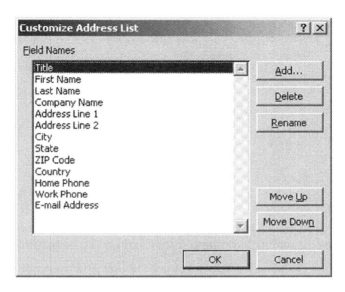

9. All the commonly used field names are displayed under **Field Names**.

  a. If you see any field names you won't use in your main document, select the name from the list, and then click **Delete** option. In this case, let us select "Country" from the list and then click **Delete.** After that, feel free to delete "Title," "Company Name," "E-mail Address," and "Work Phone."

  b. To add a field name that isn't listed, click **Add** and when the following screen appears, type the name in the box below **Type a name for your field** and then click **Ok.**

  Add the following field names one-by-one:

Prefix	Clinician	Therapist
PrimDiagnosis	SecDiagnosis	AdmDate
DateOfBirth	SSNumber	PrimCarePhy
ClinAvailability	ClinPhoneNumber	TherpAvailability
TherpPhoneNumber		

Don't forget to delete the following field names as mentioned earlier:

Title	E-Mail Address	Company
Country	Work Phone	

c. To change the sequence of field names, select a field name by clicking on it under the **Field Names**, then click the **Move Up** or **Move Down** buttons. The top-to-bottom order of the fields is the order the fields will appear for data entry in the *New Address List*. After the arrangement, click Ok to return to the *New Address List*.

10. Enter the following database one set at a time and when you finish, click **Close**

Field Name	Patient #1	Patient #2	Patient #3	Patient #4
Prefix:	Ms	Mr	Mr.	Ms
FirstName:	Maria	Ryan	Jose	Jane
LastName:	Ramos	Roberts	Santiago	Dickson
Address1:	671 Long Island Ave	2449 Street Road	9572 New Haven Road	2941 Map Rd.
Address2:	5421	B–231	C–951	D–2851
City:	Middletown	Philadelphia	Bensalem	Motown
State:	PA	PA	PA	PA
PostalCode:	1913	19031	1921	2901
HomePhone:	(215) 555-6565	(215) 555-7979	(215) 555-8989	(215) 555-1212
DateOfBirth:	11/27/1988	4/30/1990	7/21/1988	3/4/1989
SSNumber:	212-31-5423	212-45-2178	022-41-8922	021-44-6789
AdmDate:	12/4/2002	12/2/2002	1/23/2003	12/2/2002
Clinician:	E. Dada, MD	E. Balogun, MD	L. Ginger, MD	H. Desmond, MD
ClinAvailabiligy:	M–F (9:00–4:00)	M–F (9:00–4:00)	M–F (9:00–4:00)	M–F (9:00–4:00)
ClinPhoneNumber:	215-777-9192	215-777-9193	215-777-9194	215-777-9191
Therapist:	Liz Catherine	Mike Luther	M. Fukushima	M. Sukukowa
TherpAvailability:	M–F (9:00–7:00)	M–F (9:00–7:00)	M–F (9:00–7:00)	M–F (9:00–7:00)
TherpPhoneNumber:	215-777-8283	215-777-8284	215-777-8285	215-777-8282
PrimDiagnosis:	ADHD	ADHD	PTSD	OCD
SecDiagnosis:	ODD	ODD	Depressive Disorder NOS	None
PrimCarePhy:	L. Dada, MD	J. Santiago, MD	N. Gubloan	D'Angelo, MD

11. You would be returned to the following screen:

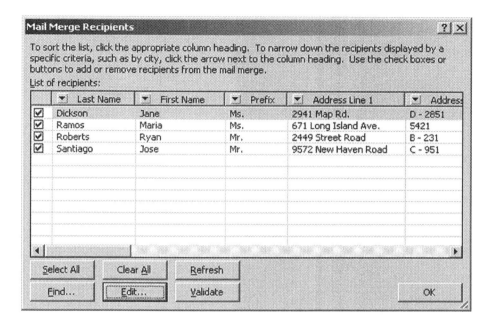

12. Check the accuracy of your data list and if they are entered correctly, click **Ok**. You would be returned to your main document with the *Mail Merge Task Pane* still showing.

Inserting Merge Fields to your Document

1. Once you have completed the development of your ***data list*** for your mail merge, you are ready to insert ***merge fields*** in the main document. Merge fields are the variable information that changes for each document. The document could be a letter, envelope, labels, fax, invoice, or agreement, or any document such as a newsletter or even a brochure. Position the insertion point where you want a merge field to appear. In this case, position your cursor (the insertion point) two spaces below the date.

Steps

2. The Mail Merge Task Pane, should look like the following:

3. Click **More items** to activate the following screen:

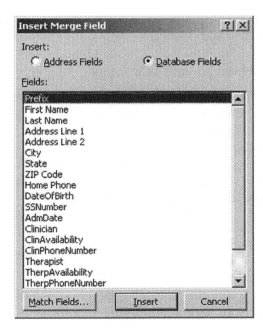

4. Click **Prefix** under *Fields* and then click **Insert**

5. In our case, we are going to start inserting the following field names exactly as they are written below:

> February 17, 2005
>
> «Prefix» «First_Name» «Last_Name»
> «Address_Line_1»
> «Address_Line_2»
> «City», «State» «ZIP_Code»
>
> Dear «Prefix» «Last_Name»

6. On the Insert Merge Field dialogue box, click on **Prefix → Insert → Close**. Hit the spacebar on your keyboard to create space and then click **More items** again.

7. Click **First Name → Insert → Close**. Hit the spacebar on your keyboard to create space and then click **More items** again.

8. Click **Last Name → Insert → Close**. Hit the spacebar on your keyboard to create space and then click **More items** again.

9. Insert the rest exactly like the example above

10. In the first paragraph of the letter, insert the field name for both the **Clinician** and the **Therapist** exactly as you see it in the following example. When you finish, your main document should look exactly like the one below. You do not have to bold the field names.

If you insert an address block field or a greeting line (otherwise know as the salutation) field into your document, you will be prompted to choose formatting style that you prefer. For example, if you click the **Greeting Line,** the following dialog box is expected to open.

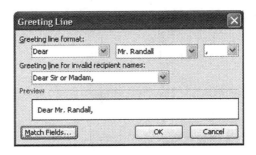

Use the lists under **Greeting line format** to make your choices. Click **Ok** when you are done.

MidMed©

2449 Golf Road
Philadelphia, PA 19131
Voice (215) 555-1212
Fax (215) 555-6767

January 23, 2003

«Prefix» «First_Name» «Last_Name»
«Address_Line_1»
«Address_Line_2»
«City», «State» «ZIP_Code»

Dear «Prefix» «Last_Name»:

This is to remind you of your previously schduled appointment with «**Clinician**» for Medication check on Thursday, January 29, 2003 at 10:30 am, and also with «**Therapist**» for psychotherapy at 11:00 am. You are hereby adviced to arrive early. Your total time at the clinic is expected to be 1½ hours.

If you have any questions or concerns, or you are going to be late for whatever reasons, feel free to call me at (215) 999-6161 or call your Psychiatrist and Therapist directly. Their numbers are as following:

When coming, kindly remember to bring the followng with you:

Insurance card
Social Security card; and
Photo identification

Sincerely,

Maria Villanueva
Secretary

cm
Enclosure
c: Front Desk Personnel

"If you want the rainbow, you have to put up with the rain."

Unknown

Chapter Five

Document Editing and Formatting

Objectives

When you finish this chapter, you will be able to:

- Highlight text using the Keyboard, Mouse and Shortcut commands

- Undo and Redo an action using Toolbars, Menu options and Shortcut commands

- Insert symbols using the numeric keypad and Menu options

- Go back to where you left off in large Word document using Shortcut without scrolling

- Perform other editing functions such as Spell Check, Bullet and Numbering

The time to correct our mistakes, and produce an error free document has come. In Microsoft Office, you can copy or cut information from within a document and paste it at a different location in the same document. You can also do the same thing between documents, or even between two different applications in Microsoft Office or any application compatible with any of the Microsoft Office applications.

Before we do anything with our project, there is some useful tips I want you to fully understand regarding document editing and formatting. To handle the tasks before us quickly and professionally, we are going to go over some basics. These include highlighting, deleting and replacing, copy or cut and paste including undo, redo and more.

Let us begin by learning "selecting" or "highlighting" text. I want you to bear in mind that when you see "selecting" mentioned, I am basically referring to "highlighting." In this case, both "selecting" and "highlighting" will be referred to interchangeably.

How to highlight text

Steps

1. Press and hold down the **left** mouse button. Move the mouse pointer to the other end of the text. Release the mouse button only when the text you want to select is highlighted.

2. Place the cursor at the beginning of the text you want to highlight. Press and hold down the **Shift** key with one finger while holding down the **right arrow** key with another finger. Release both when the text you want to select is highlighted.

3. If the cursor is blinking at the end of the word you want to highlight, press and hold down the **Shift** key with one finger while holding down the **left arrow** key with another finger. Release both when the text you want to select is highlighted.

4. To select a word, place the mouse (the "I" beam) anywhere on the word to be highlighted. Double click the left mouse button. The word you selected is now highlighted.

5. To select or highlight an entire line of text, place the cursor at the beginning of the line you want to highlight, press and hold down the **Shift** key and press the **End** key once, or place the cursor at the end of the line you want to highlight, press and hold down the **Shift** key and press the **Home** key once.

6. To select or highlight an entire document, choose **Edit → Select All,** or hold down the **Ctrl** key and press **A** once.

7. To remove highlight without deleting the highlighted text, <u>do not</u> press any key on the keyboard other than the arrow key—whichever one.

Cut and Paste.

Steps

1. Select (highlight) the information you want to move. In this case, we are going to highlight all of the second paragraph

2. Press **Ctrl + X** or click the **Cut** button on the Standard toolbar, or simply choose **Edit → Cut.**

3. Move the insertion point (the cursor) to two spaces below "Photo identification."

4. Press **Ctrl + V** or click the **Paste** button on the Standard toolbar or choose **Edit → Paste**

Notepad

To quickly move text or graphics to another location in the same document, select the information you want to move. Move the mouse pointer onto the selected area and drag the selection to the new or desired location. This feature is called drag and drop.

Delete

1. Place the cursor at the beginning of the word you want to erase

2. Press the **delete key** to erase the first letter

3. **Continue to press the delete key** until everything you want to erase is gone.

Backspace

1. Place the cursor at the end of the word you want to erase

2. Press the **backspace** key and it will back over the letter and erase it

3. **Continue to press the backspace key** until everything you want to erase is gone

Notepad

The backspace key and the delete key differ from the arrow keys. Arrow keys allow you to move up, down, left or right within a document. They **do not change** or cause changes to be made to the document. If you are trying to make changes, the backspace and delete keys are developed to **actually make changes** in your document. The **delete** key will erase or delete text to the **right** of the cursor. The **backspace** key will erase or delete text to the **left** or backward direction of the cursor.

Highlight and Replace

1. Highlight or select the block of text you want to replace

2. Start to type the new text (you don't have to delete before you start typing).

3. As soon as you press the first key of the new text, the highlighted block will be deleted

4. As you type, the new text will be inserted

The Undo and Redo Button

- In case you mistakenly erase or delete a text or graphic, <u>don't panic</u>. Simply click on the **Undo** button, or choose **Edit → Undo**, or simply hold down the **Ctrl** key and press **Z**. This will only undo the last action or changes made to your document.

- **Undo** will work an unlimited number of times, recalling in sequence changes made to a document.

- If your actions are not made in error, always feel free to use the **Redo** button, or choose **Edit → Redo** or simply hold down the **Alt + Shift** and press **Backspace**.

Format Text Using **Bold** <u>Underline</u>, and *Italic*

- To **Bold**, first highlight the text you want to bold. Click on **B** button in the toolbars or simply hold down the **Ctrl** key and press **B**. You will be able to see the bolded text as soon as the highlight is removed.

- <u>To Underline a text</u>, highlight the text you want to underline. Click on <u>U</u> button in the toolbars or simply hold down the **Ctrl** key and press U.

- *To italicize a text,* highlight the text you want to italicize. Click on *I* button or simply hold down the **Ctrl** key and press *I*.

- **Remove Bold, <u>Underline,</u> and *Italics*.** You will basically have to do what you did to create the **Bold, <u>Underline,</u> and *Italics***

Using the Keyboard to highlight

There are so many reasons you will need to select (highlight) information. Perhaps you just want to replace information, change the character or paragraph format, copy, move, or delete information. As with most *Windows* applications, *Word* works on the "select, then move, replace or delete" principle. When you highlight an area, you are shifting focus into the highlighted area. Any action performed will only affect that area only.

Steps

1. Move the insertion point (cursor) to the beginning of the text you want to select.

2. Use one of the key combinations in the following tables to select the text.

Highlight Text Using the Arrow Keys

Key	Resulting Action
Shift + ↓ [Down arrow] or ↑ [Up arrow]	Highlight one line at a time
Shift + → [Right arrow] or Shift + ← [Left arrow]	Highlight one character at a time
Shift + Ctrl + → or Shift + Ctrl + ←	Highlight one word at a time
Shift + Ctrl + ↓ or Shift + Ctrl + ↑	Highlight one paragraph at a time

Highlight Text Using the Home and End Keys

Key	Resulting Action
Shift + Home	Highlight from the insertion point (cursor point) to the beginning of the current line
Shift + End	Highlight from the insertion point to the end of the current line
Shift + Ctrl + Home	Highlight from the insertion point to the beginning of the document
Shift + Ctrl + End	Highlight from the insertion point to the end of the document
Ctrl + A	Highlight the entire document, regardless of where the insertion point is

Other Useful Shortcuts

Key	Resulting Action
Ctrl + L	Align Left
Ctrl + E	Center
Ctrl + R	Align Right
Ctrl + J	Justify
Ctrl + F	Find and Replace
Ctrl + G	Go to page, line, section, etc.
Ctrl + Backspace	Delete a word to the left
Ctrl + Y or simply press F4	Repeat your last action
Ctrl + Home	Go to the beginning of a document
Ctrl + End	Go to the end of a document
Shift + F7	Open the Thesaurus
Ctrl + K	Insert a hyperlink
Ctrl + Z	Undo
Alt + Shift + Backspace	Redo

We are now ready to edit our document. Move the cursor to the beginning of the second paragraph and highlight the entire paragraph. After that, click on the **Cut** button or choose **Edit → Cut.**

After that, move your cursor to the new location where you want to place the new text. In this case, move the cursor to two spaces below the following line:

"Photo identification"

Spell Check

1. Move the mouse pointer over to the misspelled word and right-click the mouse. Choose and click on the correct spelling, or

2. Choose **Tools → Spelling and Grammar**

3. When you see the correct spelling in the **Suggestions** box of the *Spelling and Grammar* window, click to select it and then click **Change** to make the correction.

4. Another way to correct your spelling error(s) is to move the mouse over to the misspelled word and **Right-click** the mouse. You will see a pop-up window showing what the correct spelling should be. Click on the correct spelling to accept, thereby correcting the error, or

5. You can correct the same spelling error quickly without checking the entire document using a much more faster and efficient way than the one stated in step 4 above. To find the next misspelled word in the document, press **Alt + F7**. You will see a pop-up window showing what the correct spelling should be, click on the correct spelling to accept.

Bullets and Numbering

Highlight the three items you are asking patients to bring next time they are coming to see their doctors. They are as follows:

Insurance card
Social Security card, and
Photo identification

Highlight all three and click **Numbering** button on the Standard toolbars, or simply choose **Format → Bullets and Numbering**. On the *Bullets and Numbering* window, click **Numbered** tab and select number format you like and then click **Ok.**

Insert Date

1. Choose **Insert → Date and Time** and pick the date and time in the format of February 7, 2003. Or

2. Simply press **Alt + Shift + D**. This method will produce a date in this format: **2/17/2005**

Insert Accent or Special Character such as ½, ©, č, à and more

1. Click where you want to insert the accent or character.

2. Choose **Insert → Symbol...**and when the following **Symbol** window pops up.

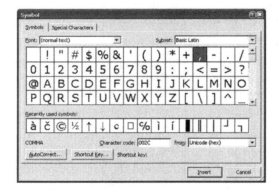

3. Scroll through it to pick the symbol of your choice.

4. Click Insert and then click Close.

Insert the symbol using the numeric keypad.

5. Simply complete step one and move on to step five

6. Make sure the **Num Lock** is on.

7. Hold down the **ALT** key, and then, using the numeric keypad, type the character code.

Here are some commonly used codes:

Word 2000 Codes	Word XP & 2003 Codes	Result
Alt + Ctrl + C	Alt + Ctrl + C	©
171	0189	½
130	0224	À
129	0252	Ü

When you finish, your document should look like the following:

MidMed©

2449 Golf Road
Philadelphia, PA 19131
Voice (215) 555-1212
Fax (215) 555-6767

January 23, 2003

«Prefix» «First_Name» «Last_Name»
«Address_Line_1»
«Address_Line_2»
«City», «State» «ZIP_Code»

Dear «Prefix» «Last_Name»:

This is to remind you of your previously scheduled appointment with «Clinician» for Medication check on Thursday, January 29, 2003 at 10:30 am, and also with «Therapist» for psychotherapy at 11:00 am. You are hereby advised to arrive early. Your total time at the clinic is expected to be 1½ hours.

When coming, kindly remember to bring the following with you:

1. Insurance card
2. Social Security card; and
3. Photo identification

If you have any questions or concerns, or you are going to be late for whatever reasons, feel free to call me at (215) 999-6161 or call your Psychiatrist and Therapist directly. Their numbers are as follows:

Sincerely,

Maria Villanueva
Secretary

cm
Enclosure
c: Front Desk Personnel

Going back to where you left off in Word Documents

Working on a long document can sometimes require that you stop to do something else such as look for more information or simply take a break. When this happens, it's easy to lose track of the exact page and paragraph where you left off. With Microsoft Word documents, picking up where you left off is very easy to do. It does not require special formatting or complicated steps. All you need to do is hold down the **Shift** key and press **F5**. The system will take you to where you were before you left to go grab a cup of coffee or make that important phone call. Don't forget, the magic is **Shift + F5**. Oh, one more thing, you can do the **Shift + F5** until you reach the location you want out of your last two locations.

Let us save what we have done so far before moving on to something new. Make sure you save both the data source and your letter. If you are trying to exit Word and dialog window pops up asking "Do you want to save changes to 'database file name'", click **Yes** to save the data source and also click **Yes** to save your document.

> "We fear things in proportion to our fear of them"
>
> Titus Livius

Chapter Six

Internet Integration and Sending Fax

Objectives

When you finish this chapter, you will be able to:

- Send E-mail as attachment
- Create and send a fax
- Create envelopes and mailing labels using the Mail Merge Wizard
- Find records in Mail Merge
- Merge document with data source

We need to have Ms. Jones review what we have done so far. As you know, Ms. Jones is very busy. It is impossible to have her come to the location where we are currently helping her Secretary to complete this project. Instead, we are going to send a copy of our letter to Ms. Jones for review and corrections (if any).

Make sure that the edited copy of the patient letter is up on your screen before completing the following steps. However, there are some issues to consider before we are ready to go ahead and send our file to Ms. Jones. First and foremost is the need to keep different versions of the same document. Why would we want to do that? One reason may be to be able to look back and see the evolution of our document. Another reason may be just to have different snapshots of our document moment by moment. Whatever the reason, we are going to save the copy we are about to send to Ms. Jones as our first version and when we receive a corrected copy back from Ms. Jones, we are going to save that one as another version. I want you to bear in mind that you can do this if you are writing a document longer than one page. You can do this if you are intending to write a book. To save our letter as a different version, follow the steps below:

Steps

1. Choose **File** → **Versions** and that should bring out the *Versions* window.

2. Click **Save Now…**and when the *Save Version* window pops up.

3. Typing a comment in the **Comment on version** box is optional.

4. Click **Ok.**

We can now go ahead and send our document (or file) to Ms. Jones. We are going to send our document via e-mail as an attachment or via fax.

E-mail attachment steps

1. If you are not currently online, make sure you do so. It'll be very difficult to complete this without Internet access (if you don't have Internet access, don't worry about it. You can always come back to try this portion of the book). Not only that, make sure your Microsoft Outlook is running as either the default mail client or alternative mail client (this is necessary and required for a smooth collaboration). If your Microsoft Outlook is not configured as the default mail client, you are likely to receive the following warning:

2. Choose **File** → **Send To** → **Mail Recipient** (**as Attachment**). If you are using Microsoft Office XP, it is advisable to click on **Mail Recipient** (**for Review**). And from the following window:

3. Type Ms. Jones' **e-mail address** in the input box across from **To:**

4. The body of your message should read "Please review the attached document." Always feel free to add more to this message if you have to. Otherwise, click **Send** to complete.

Creating and Sending a Fax

Microsoft Word 2000 as well as Microsoft Word XP includes features to help you create and send a fax. If your fax is already set up and the fax recipients are listed in your address book, you can use the Fax Wizard to look up the recipients' fax numbers. The Fax Wizard is 100% compatible with the following types of electronic address books:

• Microsoft Outlook Address Book or Contact List

• The Personal Address Book

If you have a fax program installed on your computer, you can use the Fax Wizard to create a cover sheet for the document you are about to fax and then send the cover sheet and the document from within Word.

To create and send a document and cover sheet

1. Make sure the document you want to send is currently active on your screen.

2. While the document is open, start the Fax Wizard and then choose **File** → **Send To**, and then click **Fax Recipient**.

The Fax Wizard leads you through the process of creating a cover sheet and then sending the cover sheet and your document.

Windows XP

If your computer is equipped with Windows XP, you may have to install **Fax Services** before you can send your document to Ms. Jones or to anyone else for that matter (unless it has been installed). To install **Fax Services**, follow the steps below but make sure you have your original Windows XP Professional CD as well as your Microsoft Office CD around just in case the system requests for either one or both.

To Install Fax Services in Windows XP

1. Click **Start** → **Control Panel** → **Add or Remove Programs**.

2. Look to right of the screen that pops up after you click on Add or Remove Programs and click on **Add/Remove Windows Components** and that should activate the following screen.

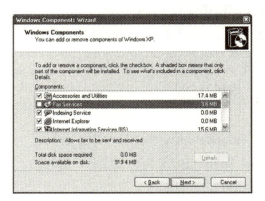

3. The fact that there is no check mark next to your **Fax Services** clearly indicates that the fax services have never been installed. If that is the case, click the check box next to **Fax Services** to select it, and then

4. Click **Next.** From this point on, carefully follow the Installation instructions on the screen. The system will no doubt ask you for your Windows XP CD and again for your Microsoft Office CD. It is advisable to have both ready.

5. When the installation of fax services is completed, and you see the following screen, click **Finish.**

Now that your fax is installed, the next thing is to start using it. Let us go ahead and fax your document.

1. Choose **File → Print** and that should take you to the following print screen:

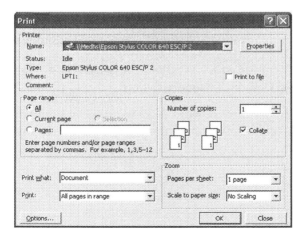

2. Click on the little box facing **Name:** to select your fax. After that, click **Ok.** The system should activate the following Send Fax Wizard.

3. Click **Next.** Please make sure you have the recipient information such as Name, Fax Number, and even the Subject matter of your fax message ready for the wizard to do a good job.

4. The "**Send Fax Wizard**" should lead you to the Fax Monitor screen. Click **More >>** to see the status of your fax. When the fax is completed, simply close the Fax Monitor.

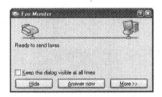

If Your Computer Does Not Support Faxing

You can use the Fax Wizard in Word 2000 to create and print cover sheets. You can then send the cover sheets and documents to recipients by using a stand alone fax machine.

Create and print a cover sheet

1. On the **File** menu, click **New.**

2. Click the **Letters and Faxes** tab.

3. Double-click the **Fax Wizard.**

Creating Envelopes — mail merge

Before we completely leave the subject of mail merge, there are two things we have to do. First, we need to create envelope and mailing labels for our mail merge. With the *Mail Merge Helper*, we can create mail merge envelopes and labels designed to use the same data source (database) as the letter we created.

We are going to use the data source created earlier. It just doesn't make sense to create a different data source.

 If you are using Clinical Solution software that allows you to integrate with Microsoft Office, you do not need to create a separate data source or database from scratch.

Notepad

Steps

1. With the main document active, choose **Tools** → **Letters and Mailings** → **Mail Merge Wizard**. From the *Mail Merge Task Pane—Step 1 of 6*, click the radio button next to **Envelope** and click **Next: Starting Document.**

2. From Step 2 of 6 of the *Mail Merge Task Pane*, click the radio button next to **Change document layout** and click **Next: Select recipients**. And you will see the following screen:

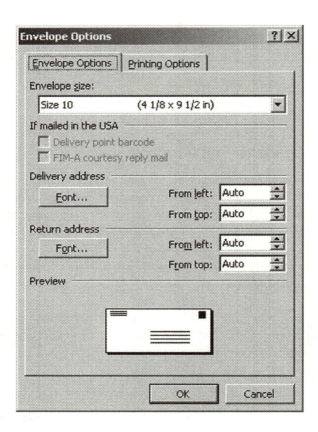

3. On the *Envelope Options* screen, click **Ok**. If you have been doing this while your letter is still active, you will see a prompt designed to let you know that the content of your current active window will be deleted. Click **Ok**

4. When your envelope screen appears, the cursor should be blinking at the top left corner where the sender's address is supposed to go. Type your address in the following format:

    Your company's name (the MidMed address)
    Street number and name
    Suite number (if applicable)
    City, State Zip Code

5. From the *Step 3 of 6*, click **Next: Arrange your envelope**

6. From Step 4 of 6, click and highlight the recipient address area of your envelope, and click **Address block**. Click **Next: Preview your envelopes**

7. From Step 5 of 6, click **Next: Complete the merge**.

8. Go to the **File** menu and click **Save As** to save your envelope with a different name. The importance of this action cannot be over emphasized.

9. Click **File → Close** to leave the envelope screen.

Create Mailing Labels

If you don't want to print recipient names and addresses directly onto each envelope, mailing labels is another choice. You can design a form that prints multiple labels on a page similar to the way you design a form letter. Again, we are going to use the same data source for our mailing labels.

Steps

1. Open any of the last documents (letter or envelope) you created and choose **Tools → Letters and Mailings → Mail Merge Wizard** and click **Next: Starting document**—Step 1 of 6.

2. From Step 2 of 6, select **Change document layout** under *Selecting starting document* and click **Next: Select recipients**. When the following screen appears, scroll down to select your appropriate label size and click **Ok**.

3. On the warning screen that follows, click **Ok**.

4. From Step 3 of 6, click **Using an existing list** and at the bottom, click **Next: Arrange your labels**.

5. From Step 4 of 6, click the Address block and when the following screen appears, click Ok.

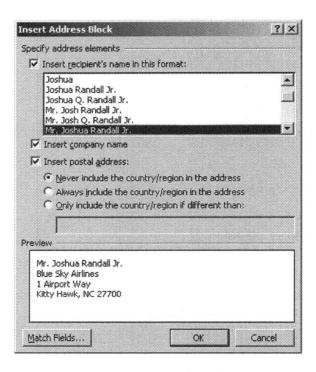

6. While you are still on Step 4 of 6, click **Update all labels** and then click **Next: Preview your labels**.

7. Step 5 of 6 should reflect the number of names and addresses in your database. To add more, click **Edit recipient list → Edit**. When you are done, click **Ok**.

8. While you are still on Step 5 of 6, click **Next: Complete the merge**.

9. Go to the **File** menu and click **Save As** to save your envelope with a different name. The importance of this action cannot be over emphasized.

10. Click **File → Close** to leave the envelope screen.

Finding Records in mail merge

Why would you want to find a specific record? Perhaps the address of a patient has changed. Or perhaps you received a "Return to Sender" notice from your last mailing. There are so many reasons you would want to find specific records in your mail merge. Regardless, all you need to do to locate the record is follow these steps.

Steps

1. Open any of the documents you created earlier—letter, envelope or labels. Click **Tools → Letters and Mailings → Mail Merge Wizard.**

2. From Step 3 of 6, click **Edit recipient list...**and on the *Mail Merge Recipients* window, click **Edit.** From the next window, click **Find Entry** and the following window will appear:

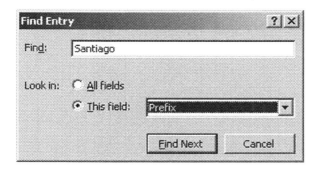

3. Type the last name of the patient you are looking for and click to select the radio button next to **This field,** use the little arrow to the right of that field to select **Last Name** and then click **Find Next.**

Merging Document with Data Source

Once you have created your main document and entered necessary information into your *Data List* (Database), and you are ready to print, always make sure the letter or document you want to print is currently active on your screen.

Steps

1. Choose **Tools → Letters and Mailings → Mail Merge Wizard.**

2. From Step 6 of 6, click print and when the following screen pops up.

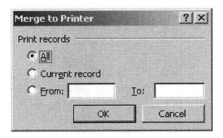

3. Make your selection appropriately and click **Ok**.

4. Make sure your printer is turned on and appropriately connected. From the Print window, click **Ok**.

"What the mind of man can conceive
and believe, it can achieve."

Napoleon Hill

Chapter Seven

Understanding Toolbars

Objectives

When you finish this chapter, you will be able to:

- Create a Toolbar
- Display or hide Toolbars
- Add Toolbar buttons

Toolbars are more like mouse shortcuts to most program features. In addition to the **Standard** toolbars, there are in excess of 15 additional toolbars in *Word 2000* and over 20 additional toolbars in *Word XP* that you can use to quickly access most of *Microsoft Word* features. Like the menu in *Word 2000 and XP*, toolbars are also adaptive and may change depending on how often you use them.

Create a New Toolbar

You may want to create your own custom toolbar showing only the buttons required for the specific tasks that you frequently perform. If you use a document that has unique formatting and perhaps printing requirements such as the mail merge document we just created, you can create a new toolbar with just those buttons to avoid having to go through the long and time consuming steps.

Steps

1. **Right-click** any toolbar, then choose **Customize**. Or click **Tools** → **Customize**. Either way should lead you to the **Customize** screen which shows the following three tabs: "Toolbars," "Commands," and "Options." Click the **Toolbars** tab.

2. Choose **New** button and that should activate the following screen:

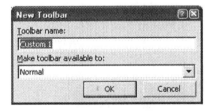

3. In the **Toolbar** Name text box, type *"My Office"* without the quotation marks as the name of your new toolbar; then click **Ok**.

4. Scroll down the list of toolbars in the **Toolbar** tab and you should see the new toolbar you just created.

Very soon, I'm going to show you how to create new buttons to help you access your document and data source (database) faster than ever before. However, to add any of the existing buttons such as the **Save All** and **Close All** to the new toolbar you just created (this way you will not have to hold down **Shift** key when you click on **File** to activate those hiding menu options) follow these steps:

5. To add any of the existing buttons to your new toolbar, click the **Commands** tab in the **Customize** dialog window.

6. In the **Categories** list box, select the category that includes the command you want the button to perform—in this case, click on **File**. Find the button that says *"Save All"* in the **Commands** list, and then **drag** that button to the new toolbar. Release the mouse button.

7. **Repeat Step 4** for each additional button such as *"Close All"* you want to add to the new toolbar. Your new toolbar will expand as you continue to add buttons. When you are finished, click **Close**.

After you create a new toolbar, you can move or resize it just as you can move or resize Word's predefined toolbars.

Display or Hide Toolbars

When you start Word, by default, the Standard and Formatting toolbars are the only toolbars likely to appear on your screen. The general consensus is that no matter what, you are bound to use these toolbars when you work in Word. There are several additional toolbars you can display when you need them. Sometimes, different toolbars will automatically appear on-screen when you are performing certain procedures. For example, when you are recording Macro, the Stop Recording toolbar appears on-screen. To help you identify which toolbar(s) are currently displayed on-screen, when you click **View**, and then **Toolbars** you will see a check mark next to each toolbar currently on-screen.

The choice to display more than the Standard and Formatting toolbars is entirely up to the individual user. Once a toolbar is activated, you can move it to virtually any location but it is much more logical to keep them well organized around the Standard toolbars which are located underneath your main menus. To display each toolbar, follow these steps:

1. Click **View** → **Toolbars** and this will bring up the list of available toolbars. Pick one-by-one those you will like to display up on your screen, or

2. Move your mouse to the toolbar area and **Right-click** the mouse on any toolbar, and then click **the name of the toolbar** you want to display.

To hide a toolbar

1. Click **View → Toolbars.** Clicking on the toolbar you want to hide will remove the previously placed check mark thereby taking it out of view, or

2. **Right-click any toolbar**, then click **the name of the toolbar** you want to hide.

Notepad

If the toolbar is a floating toolbar, you can hide it by clicking the **Close** button in the toolbar's title bar.

Add Toolbar Buttons

If you frequently use a command that is not represented on a Word toolbar, you can easily add a button to a toolbar that performs the command. If there is no room to add a button to an existing toolbar, you can remove an existing button on a toolbar that you don't use or you can create a new toolbar.

Steps

1. Display the toolbar that you want to add a button to, if necessary.
2. Choose **Tools → Customize**; then click the **Commands** tab.
3. In the Categories list box, select the category that includes the command you want the button to perform.
4. Find the button you want in the **Commands** list, and then **drag** that button to where you want the toolbar button to appear on the displayed toolbar. Release the mouse button.
5. Click **Close** to close the Customize dialog window.

Notepad

To remove a button from a toolbar, display the toolbar that includes the button you want to remove. Choose **Tools → Customize**; then click the **Commands** tab. **Drag** the button off the toolbar; then click **Close**. To reset a toolbar to its original configuration, choose **Tools → Customize**; then click the **Toolbars** tab. Select the toolbar you want to reset, and then click the **Reset** button. Click **Ok** to confirm the procedure; then click **Close** to close the dialog window.

"Few are those who see with their own
eyes and feel with their own hearts."

Albert Einstein

Chapter Eight

Recording Macro—the beginning of automation

Objectives

When you finish this chapter, you will be able to:

- Record and run macros

- Assign a macro to a button

- Protect documents from Macro Viruses

- Create easy access to a frequently used documents

There are some tasks that are just too long and at times too technical to repeat over and again. In a busy environment, such a lengthy and highly involved task may often result in human error unless something is done to reduce the possibility of unnecessary mistakes.

Any environment where employees are overworked and underpaid will surely lead to low morale and high rate of turnover. It appears that the programmers behind the development of Microsoft Office are not unaware of this fact. They are also aware of the fact that having too many people on the same assignment can at times lead to unnecessary duplications that if not properly handled in a professional way can lead to personality clashes.

In order to make the work environment less intimidating, less conflicting and error-prone, we are going to employ the use of macro to help us accomplish some of these tasks effectively and efficiently without making too much demand on anyone's time and expertise. I have to warn that the explanation given here with regard to automating Mail Merge steps works better with *Microsoft Office 97 and 2000* more so than *XP and 2003*. For that reason, the mail merge interface explains here are from *Microsoft Office 97 and 2000*. It may not work with your latest version. Log on to www.mednetservices.com to download working with mail merge in *Microsoft Office 97 and 2000* now for free.

Macro provides a means to create mini-automation without getting into all the nitty-gritty of programming. A macro provides a way to record a set of instructions that can be played back at a later time. Word's macro is capable of recording keystrokes and any associated command necessary to perform a task.

If playing back the macro results in another lengthy step, what good is it? A macro should be designed to save time and effort, thereby increasing productivity. We are going to learn the steps necessary to record macro, assign that macro to a keystroke and the same keystroke to an object like a toolbar button we can click in order to make playing it back as smooth as it can possibly be.

Recording Macros—Office 97 & 2000

Please bear in mind that our goal is to find a way to reduce the number of steps required to access what we have created so far. Needless to say, we went through a lot of steps to create our data source, but do we really need to go through the same long process just to add more information? Not if we can avoid it. If that is the case, I'm going to show you how we can program everything into a toolbar button. Did I just mention program? I did not mean to scare you in any way, shape, or form. However, there is a program included with your Microsoft Office known as Visual Basic for Application (VBA). Believe it or not, there is no better way to automate or customize program features in Microsoft Office. But when the time comes, I will expose you to the beauty of VBA. As you will soon discover, when you record a macro in Word or any program, you are in a way creating a Visual Basic for Application module with programming instructions. However, because the subject of VBA is beyond the scope of this book, I'll refrain from covering it further. For now, let's go ahead and deal graciously with the subject before us and that is recording macros. The steps you are about to perform is applicable to *Word 97 & Word 2000*.

Before you perform the following steps, make sure the mail merge letter you created earlier is opened and active on your computer screen.

Steps

1. Choose **T̲ools** → **M̲acro** → **R̲ecord New Macro**. In the **M̲acro Name** text box, type a name for the macro.

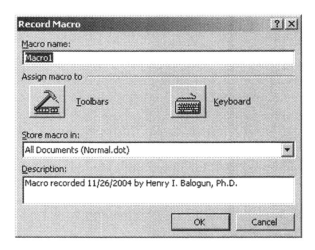

2. In the **S̲tore Macro In** box, click to select the location where you want to store the macro. If you want a macro to be available whenever you use Word, select the **All Documents (Normal.dot)** option.

3. First of all, to assign a shortcut key to the macro, click the **Keyboard** button and that should activate the following screen:

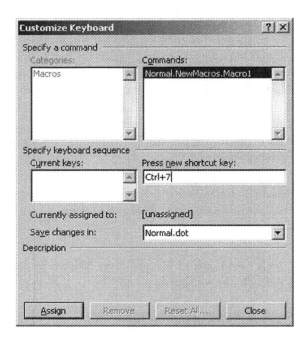

4. Make sure your cursor is blinking in the box labeled **Press New Shortcut Key**. Hold down **Alt**, or **Ctrl** key and press a letter or any number. For the sake of our project, let us hold down the **Ctrl** key and press 7. Our shortcut should read **Ctrl + 7** in the **Press New Shortcut Key** box. The inscription beneath it should read "Currently assigned to [unassigned]." If it doesn't, try another combination until it reads "Currently assigned to [unassigned]."

5. Click the **Assign** button followed by **Close** button.

6. Now we are going to perform the actions we want the macro to record and they are as follows:

    a. Choose **Tools → Mail Merge**

    b. Under Step 2, click on **Edit** and when the name of your mail merge data source appears under **Edit**, click on the name

    c. When the **Data Form** screen appears, click **Ok**.

7. To stop recording, look for the following hanging toolbar:

8. Click on the **Stop Recording** button on the toolbar.

Running Macro

Once you have created a macro, running it is easy. When we were recording the last macro, we assigned the macro to a shortcut—Ctrl + 7. To run the macro, make sure the original mail merge letter is open and active on your screen.

Hold down the **Ctrl** key and press 7. The Data Form screen should pop up.

To run a macro from the **Tools** menu, follow these steps:

1. Open the document in which you want to run the macro—in this case, open the mail merge letter.
2. Choose **Tools** → **Macro** → **Macros**.
3. In the list box, select the macro you want to run; then click **Run** to run the macro.

Assigning a Macro to a Button

Once you have created a macro to automate repetitive tasks, you can assign the macro to a button on the toolbar to make it much easier to use.

Steps

1. Display the toolbar that you want to add the button to. We are going to add the new button to the toolbar we created earlier. Don't forget that we gave the new toolbar the name "My Office."

2. **Right-click** on the toolbars of your choice, then choose **Customize** from the shortcut menu.

3. In the **Categories** list box, select **Macros**. In the **Commands** list, find the macro you want to place on the toolbar, and then drag that new macro name to your new toolbar. Release the mouse button.

4. To change the macro name you just dragged onto your new toolbar button, right-click **the name**. <u>Do not</u> close the **Customize** dialog window while you are doing this. Then, in the **Name** text box, type or edit the name; right-click the button again and point to the **Change Button Image** command to choose an image from the displayed choices.

5. If you want to display just the image, right-click the button and select **Default Style**. Click **Close** to close the Customize dialog window.

Notepad

Feel free to visit www.mednetservices.com for lots of free downloadable files including extensive information and instructions on Recording Macro and also on Assigning a Macro to a Button and more.

Protecting Office Documents from Macro Viruses

In these days of unexpected computer viruses, one thing you seriously don't need is the one generated by the system itself either through the use of program features or conflict in applications. It is always good to know how to protect your documents from macro viruses simply by selecting an appropriate security level.

A macro virus can occur when "the macro picked up some harmful codes written in the macro language of programs" as a result of inappropriate recording of macros or when the macro is inadvertently altered. Just like any other virus out there, these viruses can do serious harm to programs and data.

To protect your document or data in Microsoft Word, Excel, and PowerPoint, it is advisable to set the security level to low, medium or high. If you fail to protect your document, Microsoft Office automatically disables macros without notice and this may render the macro you recorded ineffective.

Level of Protection

By default, Excel and PowerPoint are set to the medium security level, and Word is set to the "high" security level. Always remember to set the appropriate security level for your system.

1. **Low Security:** "When the security level is set to low, Office performs no macro checking when you open a document and enables all macros. This security level is not recommended because no protection is active when it is selected."

2. **Medium Security:** "When the security level is set to medium, you are prompted to enable or disable macros in documents when you open the documents. It is recommended that you disable a macro if you do not know who created it."

3. **High Security:** "When the security level is set to high, macros must have digital identification stamps indicating that the macros have not been altered. Otherwise, when you open a document, Office automatically disables macros without notice."

To set a security level for your computer

1. Choose **Tools** → **Macro**, and then click **Security**.

2. Click the **Security Level** tab, and then click the radio button next to a security level you prefer.

Notepad

For more information about how you can protect documents from macro viruses, go to www.mednetservices.com for lots of free downloadable files. If the file you are looking for is not available right away, all you need to do is come back again as we are constantly adding more files everyday.

Create Easy Access to Documents You Use Often

At times you need to dig deeper to find a better way to make things easier on yourself. It is easy to create a file and not remember where that file is in your system. In order to eliminate unnecessary frustration and headache, there is an option known as **Work** menu in Word that only few people know about. You can use this feature to keep an easily accessible list of your favorite Word files. This is like creating a shortcut. Your current menu options are:

File	Edit	View	Insert	Format	Tools	Table	Window	Help

We are going to add the **Work** menu to the menu bar. But before you do that, make sure there are no files currently open. It is advisable to do this the moment you start Microsoft Word.

Steps

1. On the **Tools** menu, click **Customize**, and then click the **Commands** tab.

2. In the **Categories** box, click **Built-in Menus**.

3. Click **Work** in the **Commands** box and drag it next to the Help menu.

Now that you have the Work menu in place, you can add any open Word document to your list. Let us go ahead and open the document we created earlier. Follow the steps outlined below:

1. To add the current document to the Work menu, on the **Work** menu, click **Add to Work Menu.**

2. To open a document, on the **Work** menu, click the document you want to open.

If you mistakenly add a document to your **Work** menu and you have to remove it for any reason, follow these steps to remove the document.

1. Press **Ctrl** + **ALT** + - (dash key). Your cursor will look like a large, bold underscore.

2. Click to activate **Work** menu, and

3. On the **Work** menu, click the document you want to remove.

"The most important thing is to not stop questioning."

Albert Einstein

Chapter Nine

Document Design and Translation

Objectives

When you finish this chapter, you will be able to:

- Design and translate documents
- Insert, respond and delete a comment
- Create and Print business cards
- Create tables using Keyboard commands, Menu options and Toolbars
- Format and wrap text around a table
- Perform calculations in a table

We have a feedback from the Clinical Director. Needless to say, she is very grateful for taking the time to help her Secretary in the effort to accomplish her goal. However, there are some new requests. She would like to know if it is possible to:

1. Include a table in the letter. The table should be designed to show Names, Availability and Phone Numbers of every Psychiatrist and Therapist per patient (this is indicated in the comment she inserted in the letter she sent back to us).

2. Design Business Card for every Psychiatrist and Therapist

3. Design a new:
   a. Consent to treatment
   b. Patient right
   c. Psychiatric Evaluation Form
   d. Release of Information

4. Translate every document including the letter we created a while ago, into Spanish.

Before you run undercover or take the next flight out of town, I just want to let you know that you can actually do all these using your Microsoft Word. I'm going to show you how to accomplish it in just a few minutes.

I don't want you to dwell on the illusion that once the handshake has taken place, our job is done. If anything, the handshake means that the work has just begun. But for now, let us concentrate on the task before us.

Dealing with Comment

Let me explain briefly the use of comment in Microsoft Word. In addition to the e-mail message received from the Clinical Director, she also sent back the same letter we sent to her for review. On the letter she indicated through the use of comment the precise location where changes should be made. This requires explanation as to how to use comment in Microsoft Word.

A comment is a text note that you can embed inside a Word document to indicate what changes are required and where the changes are to be made or should go. One good thing about Word comment is its ability to display, separately, the name of the author as well as the text of the comment. The following is a copy of the letter with a comment as to where we should insert table:

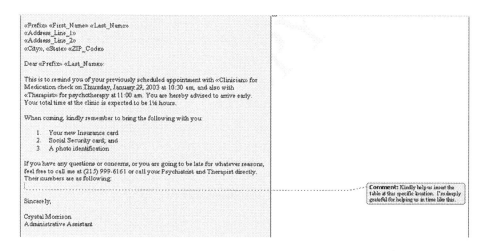

Insert a comment

1. Click the location where you want to place comment.

2. On the **Insert** menu, click **Comment**.

3. Type the comment text in the **comment balloon**.

4. In case the comment balloon is not displayed, type the comment in the **Reviewing Pane**

5. To view the name of the reviewer, move your mouse over the comment and it should display the name of the reviewer.

To respond to a comment

1. Click the existing comment, choose **Insert → Comment**.

2. Type your response in the new **comment balloon**.

To delete (remove) a comment

1. Move your mouse on the comment you want to delete and right-click the mouse

2. On the pop up menu, click **Delete comment**.

We can now go ahead to attend to the Director's request by starting with the creation and printing of a business card. Some of the ways you can create attractive and professional business card quickly using *Microsoft Word Office* is to either use ready-made business card templates from the *Microsoft Office Template Gallery*, or create one from scratch with the help of the **Envelopes and Labels** dialog window. I'm going to show you how to create one from scratch.

Create and print business cards

1. From Word 2000, choose **Tools → Envelopes and Labels** (if you are using *Word XP or 2003*, choose **Tools → Letters and Mailings** and then click **Envelopes and Labels**). Either one should take you to the following screen:

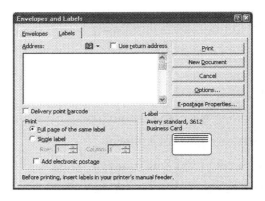

2. Click the **Labels** tab, and in the **Address** box, enter the following information about one of the Psychotherapists. Also, don't forget to enter the name of the clinic and phone number. In other words, enter the following information exactly as you see it:

> MidMed©
> Mari Fukushima, MA
> Psychotherapist
> 2449 Golf Road
> Philadelphia, PA 19131
> Voice (215) 555-1212
> Fax (215) 555-6767

3. Under **Print**, do not change the selected default which is **Full page of the same label**. This allows you to print multiple business cards on a perforated, heavyweight cardstock sheet by *Avery*.

4. Click **Options**, and the **Label Options** screen pops up,

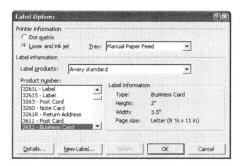

5. Click one of the radio buttons under **Printer information** to choose between **Dot matrix** or **Laser and Ink Jet** printer (whichever one you prefer—I'm quite sure your choice will be **Laser and Ink Jet**).

6. In **Label products** under **Label Information**, leave the default selected, **Avery Standard**.

7. Under **Product number**, choose the business card number corresponding to the Avery Product you are going to use. In our case, click **3612 Business Card.** Just in case the product number you want is not listed, one of the listed labels may correspond to the paper size you want. Watch out for the number as well as the paper size under **Label Information**.

8. Click **Ok**.

9. You are now back in the **Envelopes and Labels** dialog window.

10. To modify the business card, click **New Document**

11. Highlight the clinic name, choose **Format** → **Font**, and on the Font window are the following tabs: *Tab, Character Spacing* and *Text Effects* (Word XP)

12. With the **Font** tab activated, choose **Times New Roman** under **Font**, and make the **Font Style** = Bold and **Font Size** = 18, and click **Ok**.

13. After that, highlight the name and title of the Psychotherapist, and choose **Format** → **Font** to make the following changes. **Font** = Times New Roman, **Font Style** = Regular, **Font Size** = 11

14. Click **Ok.** While the name and title is still highlighted, click **Align Right** button on the **Formatting** toolbar or simply hold down the **Ctrl** and press **R**

15. Do the same to the address of the clinic but **Align Left.** Your business card should look like the following:

> **MidMed©**
>
> Mari Fukushima, MA
> Psychotherapist
>
> 2449 Golf Road
> Philadelphia, PA 19131
> Voice (215) 555-1212
> Fax (215) 555-6767

16. Copy cell one to all the 10 cells of your business card page but make sure you limit everything to only one page.

To copy from one cell and paste to another:

Move the mouse close to **the edge** of the cell you just formatted. Your mouse will appear like this =>. Move the mouse on to the edge of the line of the cell and it will change to a small solid dark arrow. When you see the solid dark arrow, click the cell to highlight it. Hold down **Ctrl** key and press **C** to copy. To paste, press the Tab key to move and highlight the next cell. When the next cell is highlighted, hold down the **Ctrl** key and press **V.**

17. To print your business card, load the Avery Business Card paper into your printer

18. Choose **File → Print.** Make sure your printer's name is displayed in the **Printer Name** box and click **Ok.** (More on printing document later on)

Notepad

I'm quite sure you can do a better design of business card than the one we did together. Experiment and practice as much as you can, and don't forget to visit www.mednetservices.com to download some Business Card templates you can use over and again.

Translate Word Document from inside Word

Translating a word, phrase or even an entire document into another language is easy to do in Microsoft Word XP than in Word 2000. This is a goal that can be accomplished by using the **Translate** task pane (available only in Word XP otherwise known as Word 2002). Not only does this provide access to many languages now available in Word, you can also use it to access the appropriate online site where you do most of your language translations effortlessly.

For those of you who are using Word XP, on the **Tools** menu point to **Language** and click **Translate**. This will activate the **Language task pane** to the right of your screen. If you are using *Microsoft Word 2003*, you will see the **Research task pane** open to the right of your screen like the one below:

From this task pane, you can:

1. Check words or phrases in the dictionary of another language, provided that the language dictionary is installed in your computer system.

2. Use the **Translate** task pane or the **Translation** in the **Research** task pane to insert translated text directly into your document.

3. Use the **Translate** task pane to access translation services on the World Wide Web, to translate a section of text or an entire document.

4. Click the **Go** button under **Translate via the Web** to translate text. You've got to be online (on the Internet) to enjoy this service.

If this is your first time using the language translator via Microsoft Word, the system will take you to the Internet site where you can install an appropriate language translator of your choice. When you click **Go**, you should see a web page showing the map of different Microsoft locations around the world. Click on the **Country** where you are and that will direct you to the appropriate web page where you can install the language translator of your choice.

5. The title of the next page should say, **Translate Within Word**

6. Pick one of the two plug-in translators currently available for Word XP (2002) to download and install. Depending on the speed of your system, downloading should not take longer than a few seconds. After the download, install the plug-in (program) right away. To use it, follow these simple steps:

    a. From your Microsoft Word, choose **Tools → Language → Translate**.

    b. You've got to be online to use the program

    c. Highlight the area of your document to translate

    d. Click the box under **Translate via the Web** in the **Translate** task pane.

    e. Pick a language of your choice. Example: **English (US) to Spanish (Spain)**

    f. Click **Go** and the translation begins. When you see the correct translation of your text, don't just sit there and enjoy it all alone, pick up the phone and

7. Call me in the morning and let me know that this is the best thing since sliced bread. (I'm just kidding. Don't go looking for my phone number—I don't have one).

Notepad

Ordinarily, most languages (other than English—USA and Western European) are not part of the standard installation of Microsoft Word. However, if you are going to use another language, it is advisable to install one of the two available plug-in translators for Microsoft Word XP (2002). To install language translator, follow the instruction given earlier on the previous page. If you are using Word 2000, once your document is finished and ready to be translated, use the following site (among others) for the translation:
http://www.worldlingo.com/microsoft/computer_translation.html

Before leaving the subject of language translation, I would like to give you the first and only homework. Let's see if you can translate this Yoruba language expression into English, Spanish, French and Japanese. The expression is "**Mo feran re.**" Send your response to Balogun@mednetservices.com. This is a homework assignment strictly for non-Yorubas. Yoruba speaking people are not eligible to participate. One more thing, if you can include the history (not detailed history) and culture of one of the most highly intelligent, loving and caring people on earth—the people of Ekiti, you will not only be my number one friend in the world, you will definitely win a surprise package. Good luck!

Create Tables

When it comes to organizing and formatting text and numbers or even graphics, tables are your number one means of doing it. Tables are one of Microsoft Word's most powerful and useful tools. You can use it to write movie scripts, resumes and advertising scripts. As a matter of fact, once you know how to create tables, there is no limit to what you can use it for. Tables are composed of cells like in Excel. These cells are organized in vertical columns and horizontal rows. Once a table is created, you can insert, edit, align, change line spacing, apply bullets and numbering and format your text or numbers any way you so desire. In a way, you can work within tables just as you would in a normal document.

How to create tables

1. You can use the **Insert Table** button available on the **Standard Toolbar**, or

2. Choose **Insert → Tables.** *Highlight the number of rows and columns* you want and simply **click,** or

3. You can create tables in Microsoft Word by simply typing out a string of **Plus Signs (+)** and **Minus Signs (-).** For example: When you type it exactly as you see it here; +--------------------+----------------------+--------------------------+ and press **Enter,** you should have a table consisting of one row and three columns that looks like the following:

Notepad

If you are having problems with the third step explained above, don't panic. It could be that the feature that would have made it easier for you to perform this step is not yet turned on. All you need to do is turn on this important feature in Word. To do this, choose **Tools →** **AutoCorrect** (in Word XP, it is **AutoCorrect Options**). Then, click the **AutoFormat As You Type** tab and place a check mark in the **Tables** box.

To add more rows and delete row(s)

1. Simply move your cursor to the last column of the last row (if you have more than one row) and then press the **Tab** key, or

2. Move your cursor to the end of the last row and press the **Enter** key.

3. To delete row, place the cursor in the row you want to delete, choose Table → Delete → Row.

To add and delete columns

1. Move your cursor to where you want to add a column. Choose **Table →** **Insert**, and click on **Column to the left** or **Column to the right** depending on where you want to insert the new column.

2. In Word 2000, choose **Insert → Table** and then click **Add Colums.** To delete a column, move the cursor to the column you want to delete and choose **Table → Delete → Column.**

Before we forget, let us insert a table in the letter we created earlier. At the end of the last paragraph (the paragraph before "Sincerely"), press the **Enter** key twice. After that, try one of the steps for inserting a table explained above. Insert a table consisting of three rows and three columns. Type the heading and insert merge fields as follows:

First Row:	Staff	Availability	Phone Number
Second Row:	«Clinician»	«ClinAvailability»	«ClinPhoneNumber»
Third Row:	«Therapist»	«TherpAvailability»	«TherpPhoneNumber»

Dear «Prefix» «Last_Name»:

This is to remind you of your previously scheduled appointment with «Clinician» for Medication check on Thursday, January 29, 2003 at 10:30 am, and also with «Therapist» for psychotherapy at 11:00 am. You are hereby advised to arrive early. Your total time at the clinic is expected to be 1½ hours.

When coming, kindly remember to bring the following with you:

4. Insurance card
5. Social Security card; and
6. Photo identification

If you have any questions or concerns, or you are going to be late for whatever reasons, feel free to call me at (215) 999-6161 or call your Psychiatrist and Therapist directly. Their numbers are as following:

Staff	Availability	Phone Number
«Clinician»	«ClinAvailability»	«ClinPhoneNumber»
«Therapist»	«TherpAvailability»	«TherpPhoneNumber»

Sincerely,

Maria Villanueva
Secretary
cm
Enclosure
c: Front Desk Personnel

Formatting a Table

You can format a table basically the same way you format any text—change text color, font size, and background including line spacing. We are going to format the table we just inserted into the letter. To accomplish this goal, let us:

1. Click and place the cursor in the heading row—column one of row one.

2. Hold down the **Shift** key and press the **Right Arrow** key on your keyboard until the entire row is highlighted.

3. Choose **Format → Borders and Shading…**And that will take you to the following screen:

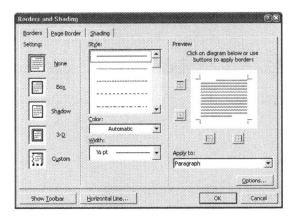

4. Click the **Shading** tab and from the forth row in the color palette, click the third column and the little box next to it should read **Olive Green** and click **Ok.**

5. While the heading is still highlighted, choose **Format → Font** and from the **Font Color**, click the last column of the last row which is **White**.

6. From the **Font Style**, click **Bold** and after that, click **Ok.**

7. To remove the highlight, press any **Arrow** key on your keyboard. After performing **Merge**, your table should look exactly like the following:

Staff	Availability	Phone Number
H. Desmond, MD	M–F (9:00–4:00)	215-777-9191
M. Sukukowa, MA	M–F (9:00–7:00)	215-777-8282

To adjust row heights and column widths

Position the mouse pointer on the gridline between columns and drag to the left to reduce the column or to the right to increase the column.

Wrap Text Around Tables

Word 2000 as well as Word XP provides new ways to wrap text around tables to create a professional looking document (I dare you to create one better than the one displayed here).

Staff	Availability	Phone Number
Dr. H. Desmond	M–F (9:00–4:00)	215-777-9191
M. Sukukowa	M–F (9:00–7:00)	215-777-8282

"Text automatically wraps around a table when you insert it on the left or right margin in a document with existing text." Bear in mind that a table that spread from left margin to the right margin will not work well with text wrap. The size of your table matters a great deal when it comes to wrapping text around tables.

To wrap text around a table

1. Click anywhere in the table. Choose **Table → Table Properties** or **Right click** on the table itself and then click **Table Properties**. Either way, when the following screen pops up

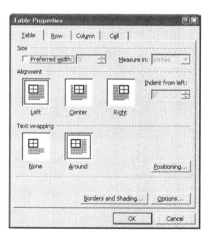

2. Click the **Table** tab. And under **Text wrapping**, click **Around**.

3. Click **Ok.**

More on this at www.mednetservices.com

Perform Calculations in a Table

Microsoft Word makes it possible to add, subtract, multiply, and divide values in table cells. One thing you really need to understand is how cells are referenced. In Microsoft Word individual table cells are referred to by the column letter and row number. Example, "A1" refers to the first column and first row while "B1" refers to the second column of the first row (just like in Excel). Let us create a table consisting of three rows and four columns table and populate the table like the one below:

256	584	217	1057
460	12	10	46
754	15	21	11310

To perform calculations

1. Make sure your cursor (the insertion point) is in cell A4 and that is column "A4" of the first row.

2. Choose **Table → Formula**. That will activate the calculation screen like the one below:

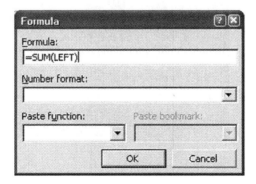

3. Under **Formula,** delete part of the automated formula. Delete the closing parenthesis and the word **Left** using backspace.

4. After the opening parenthesis, type this formula (**A1:C1**). When you are done, your formula should look exactly like **=Sum(A1:C1)**

5. Click **Ok.**

6. Move your cursor to column "D2" and choose **Table → Formula** and type the =A2/C2

7. Click **Ok.**

8. Move your cursor to column "D3" and repeat the rest of step 6 and then type =(A3)*B2

9. Click **Ok.** Your table should have the exact same numbers as the one shown below:

256	584	217	1057
460	12	10	46
754	15	21	11310

Some other formulas you can perform within tables in Microsoft Word:

Addition	=(A1)+16 or =(A1+A3)
Add a range of cells	=Sum(A1:C3)
Division	=(A2)/(C2) or =(A2)/10
Subtract two cells	=(A2-B2)
Multiplications	=(B1*B3) or =PRODUCT(B1)*(B3)

Notepad

Calculations in Microsoft Word do not necessarily work like calculations in Excel. If you add a row or column into the table you will have to manually recalculate or redefine your Word table formula. You are better off using Microsoft Excel to perform complex calculations. For more information and free downloads, go to www.mednetservices.com

"A picture is a poem without words."

Horace

Chapter Ten

Document Layout

Objectives

When you finish this chapter, you will be able to:

- Change margins, paper size, paper source, and paper layout
- Apply indentations to document
- Align text and create columns
- Apply paragraph spacing, bookmarks, and watermarks
- Create headers and footers
- Insert page numbers

In business, to say that image can sometimes make or break a business is nothing short of absolute truth. And when this basic principle is violated businesses are in a way playing the game of hit or miss with the possibility of a high risk of financial loss in the face of diminishing growth.

As you know, the goals of MidMed include increasing productivity and reducing idle time, which would eventually lead to increase in the bottom line. As for the Director, having any outside professional or consultant come in to help in time like this is unacceptable. We are going to focus our time and energy doing one thing and that is to help Ms. Jones' Secretary.

We have three important documents to prepare (Consent to Treatment, Release of Information and Patients' Right) and we cannot afford not to do a good job. Go to www.mednetservices.com to download copies. I want you to reproduce a better copy. This clinic is well known for its professionalism, and well organized environment. This is an image we are not prepared to trade for anything less than the best.

The fact of the matter is that you are going to actually produce those documents. Hey, this is nothing to sneeze about. I'm going to give you an in-depth training in design and what goes into every aspect of creating professional looking documents. First of all, let us begin by looking into:

Page Setup

Changing Margins

There is no easier way to understand page setup without recalling its properties. As you will discover, the default settings are usually one-inch top and one-inch bottom margins. Another thing is the right and left margin which by default are set at 1.25" each.

Normally, the gutter margin is zero by default, and the header and footer from the edge is one-half inch. These settings are adequate for most documents but there are some instances whereby changing any of them is imperative. Changes made because of the requirement of one document do not change the default for every document. You have the option to change these default settings on a document-by-document basis, or change them permanently. The latter is not advisable in an environment like an outpatient clinic where producing different types of documents is highly required. To change the default settings, follow these steps:

1. Choose **File** →, **Page Setup**, and that should activate the **Page Setup** properties screen.

2. Click the **Margins** tab.

3. Under Margins feel free to **increase or decrease** "Top," "Bottom," "Left," or "Right" margins. Keep an eye on the **Preview** screen to see how the margins increase or decrease.

4. Set the **Header** and **Footer** as you please. The default is usually 0.5".

5. If you will be binding the document and want the inside margin to remain constant, click **Mirror Margins**. In Word XP, under **Paper** click the box next to **Multiple Pages** to select **Mirror Margins** in order to toggle that feature on and off.

6. In the **Apply To** box, indicate what section of the document you want these changes to affect (apply).

7. If you are creating a template and you want these changes to be available to all new documents using the same template, click **Default**, and then click **Yes**.

8. Click **Ok**.

Changing Paper Size

Steps

1. Choose **File** → **Page Setup**, and then click the **Paper Size** tab. If you are using Word XP, it is simply **Paper** tab.

2. Look for and select the paper size that matches your needs from the **Paper Size** box.

3. If you cannot find your paper size in the **Paper Size** box, you can always type in the correct size in the **Width** and **Height** text boxes. Or you can simply scroll through and select sizes of your choice.

4. To pick the appropriate orientation, in **Apply To** box, indicate what section of the document you want these changes to affect (apply).

5. If you are creating a template and you want these changes to be in effect with all new documents using the same template, click **Default**, and then click **Yes**.

6. Click **Ok**.

Changing Paper Source

Steps

1. Choose **File** → **Page Setup** to display the **Page Setup** dialog window as shown on the previous page.

2. From the dialog window, select the **Paper Source** tab.

3. Under the **First Page** list box, select the location for the paper of the first page of each document you are likely to print. It is advisable to leave this as the default setting.

4. Under the **Other Pages** list box, select the location for the paper of the remaining pages you are likely to print. Again, it is advisable to leave this as the default setting.

5. In the **Apply To** box, indicate what section of the document you want these changes to affect (apply).

Changing Page Layout

If you are going to be using headers and footers, this will enable you to choose whether your headers and footers are the same all throughout the document you are creating, or change as you desire. Example: You can choose to print the header and footer on all pages except the first page. You can also specify how you want text positioned on the page. To configure the page layout, follow these steps:

1. Choose **File** → **Page Setup** to display the Page Setup dialog window, and then click the **Layout** tab.

2. Under the **Section Start** drop-down list, select where you want the new section(s) to start.

3. In the radio button next to Headers and Footers section, click the options of your choice out of the only two available: **Different Odd and Even** or **Different First Page**.

4. Under **Vertical Alignment** drop-down arrow, click to choose between **Top**, **Center**, **Justified**, or **Bottom**.

5. In the **Apply To** box, indicate what section of the document you want these changes to affect (apply).

6. If you are creating a template and you want these changes to be in effect with all new documents using the same template, click **Default**, and then click **Yes**.

7. Click **Ok**.

Indenting

Both Sides of Paragraph

Another way to add a touch of professionalism to your document is through the efficient use of indentations. The applications of indentations are for various reasons. At times, you can use it to draw the reader's attention to a specific area of a document. Margins are usually applicable to the entire document or sections within the document, but paragraph indentations apply to one or more paragraphs. To indent both sides of a paragraph, follow these steps:

1. Make sure the cursor (the insertion point) is blinking in the beginning of the paragraph you want to indent, or simply select multiple paragraphs to indent.

2. Choose **Format** → **Paragraph**, and when the following Paragraph dialog window is displayed, click the **Indents and Spacing** tab (if not already selected).

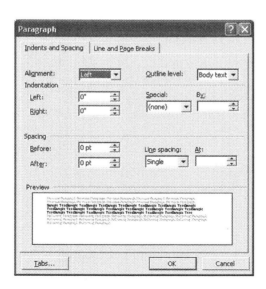

3. Under Indentation, type or select a value in the **L̲eft** and do the same thing for the **Right** box.

4. Click **Ok** to apply the indentation to the paragraph(s) you selected.

First Line

There are some people who prefer to have the first line of every paragraph of their modified block style for letters or documents indented. Regardless of the style you prefer you can use the **F̲ormat → P̲aragraph** command to indent the first line of every paragraph of your letter or document.

Steps

1. Make sure the cursor (the insertion point) is blinking in the beginning of the paragraph you want to indent, or simply select multiple paragraphs to indent.

2. Choose **F̲ormat → P̲aragraph**.

3. Click the **I̲ndents and Spacing** tab.

4. Click the box under **S̲pecial** to select **First Line**.

5. In the **By** box, type a new value or accept the 0.5" default indentation setting.

6. Click **Ok**.

Increase and Decrease Indent

You can use the Increase Indent and Decrease Indent buttons on the **Formatting** toolbar to move a paragraph inward (increase) or outward (decrease). The **Formatting** toolbar buttons by default is set at 0.5." If you have not changed Word's default tabs, you will discover that they are still set at 0.5" across the line.

Steps

1. Move the cursor to either the beginning or the end of the paragraph to be indented, or select multiple paragraphs to indent.

2. Click the **Increase Indent** button to indent the paragraph(s) 0.5" per click.

3. Click the **Decrease Indent** button to decrease the indent 0.5" per click.

Hanging Indent

When it comes to dealing with bulleted or numbered lists, glossary items, and bibliography entries, hanging indent is more appropriate. The first line of the paragraph doesn't move, while the remaining lines of the paragraph move to the right at the indent location.

Steps

1. Make sure the cursor (the insertion point) is blinking in the beginning of the paragraph you want to indent, or simply select multiple paragraphs to indent.

2. Choose **Format** → **Paragraph**.

3. Click the **Indents and Spacing** tab.

4. Click the box under **Special** to select **Hanging**.

5. In the **By** box, type a new value or accept the 0.5" default indentation setting.

6. Click **Ok**.

Adding Drop Cap

In case you are wondering what is a drop cap? A *drop cap* is a large capital letter usually of the first word of the first line of a paragraph. This large capital letter aligns with the top of the first line of the paragraph but successive line or lines (depending on the size of the capital letter) are indented for adequate space. "Drop caps usually mark the beginning of key sections or major topics in a document."

Steps

1. **Highlight the first letter** of the first word of the paragraph you want to change into a drop cap.

2. Choose **Format** → **Drop Cap** to display the Drop Cap dialog window.

3. Under **Position**, select <u>D</u>ropped.

4. In the **Options** section, select the <u>F</u>ont from the drop-down list (select Times New Roman, or any font of your choice)

5. Change the <u>L</u>ines to Drop from the default three (3) to two (2)

6. To change the distance of the text from the drop cap, use the increment buttons on the **Distance from Te<u>x</u>t** option

7. Click **Ok.**

Notepad

To remove drop caps, simply click the drop caps text, choose **F<u>o</u>rmat →** **Drop Cap**, click the **<u>N</u>one** option in the Position section of the dialog window, and then click **Ok.**

Useful Shortcuts on Indentation

Key	Shortcut
Move the left indent to the next tab stop-inward.	Ctrl + M
Move the left indent back to the preceding tab stop-outward	Ctrl + Shift + M
Create a hanging indent	Ctrl + T
Undo the hanging indent by moving back to the preceding tab	Ctrl + Shift + T
Remove indentation all together	Ctrl + Q

Alignment

By design, Word (like any other word processor) automatically aligns text to the left. Accepting this type of alignment depends on your type of document or preferences. The question then becomes "To be or not to be?" You have a choice. Some of the choices available to you include; changing the alignment to center, right, full justified, or back to left.

As you have seen in the letterhead we created earlier, the address of MidMed is aligned right. You can do the same thing for newsletters, brochures, agreement or formal business letters. The choice of which alignment is right for you is entirely up to you. Let us take a careful look at some alignment currently available in Microsoft Word.

Align Text Horizontally

To call the attention of your system to the area of your text you are going to align, you need to first select (highlight) the area. It could be a word, a phrase, paragraph or paragraphs.

On your **Formatting** toolbars, look for these  buttons: They are arranged in the following order

1. Align Left
2. Center
3. Align Right
4. Justify

To align your text, follow these steps

1. Select (highlight) the text you want to align
2. To align left press **Ctrl + L** or simply click on the button that says **Align Left**
3. To centralize press **Ctrl + E**, or click on **Center**
4. To align right press **Ctrl + R**, or click on **Align Right**
5. To justify press **Ctrl + J**, or click on **Justify**.

Align Text Vertically

If you want to deviate from the way Microsoft Word aligns text to the top margin, there is no rule against that (wow, isn't that good to know!). As far as Microsoft Word is concerned, your wish is his command. You may need to align your text a little differently, most especially if you are trying to create a report cover. To accomplish this goal, follow these simple steps

1. Move the cursor to the beginning of the text you want to align.

2. Choose **File** → **Page Setup** to display the Page Setup dialog window.

3. Click the **Layout** tab, and then click the box under **Vertical Alignment list**, and select **Center**, or **Justify**, or **Top**, or **Bottom** to change the alignment.

4. In **Apply To list** box, select whichever is appropriate, and then click **Ok**.

Insert Newspaper style Columns

Another way to beautify your document is through the use of columns. By default, the standard Word layout is newspaper style, in which all columns are the same width, and text flows from the top of the first column down to the bottom of the column unto the top of the next and continue that way until every column is populated with text page after page just like you see in this section. (If I were you I would try this over and again).

Creating Columns of Equal Width

1. Click the **View** menu to switch to **Page Layout View** (in *Word 2000 and XP-2002*, the same is known as **Print Layout View**), or you can simply click Page Layout View or Print Layout View button displays at the bottom left corner of the document window before you get to the Taskbar, you should see these buttons:

2. You can choose to format an entire document with columns, or just a section of it.

3. On the Standard toolbar, click the **Columns** ▦ button.

4. Move the **mouse pointer** to select the number of columns. The same screen should indicate the number of columns selected. Select **2 columns** and click when your mouse is on the second column. Another way to do it is:

5. Choose **Format** → **Column** and that will activate the following screen:

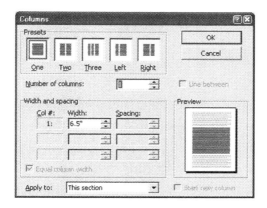

6. Click **Two** and adjust **Spacing** as you like. The default for spacing is usually 0.5"

Notepad

To insert columns in text frames, or comment boxes, and even headers and footers (if that becomes a choice for you), it is advisable to use a table. Newspaper columns are not currently available in headers and footers, comment boxes and frames of Microsoft Word.

Balancing Column Lengths

Steps

1. Make sure your cursor is blinking at the end of the text in the last column of the section you want to balance.

2. Choose **Insert** → **Break** to display the following Break dialog window:

3. Click the radio button next to **Continuous** under **Section break types** and then click **Ok.**

Create Columns of Unequal Width

Steps

1. Highlight (Select) **the text you want to format** into columns

2. Choose **Format → Columns** to display the **Columns** dialog window as in the previous page.

3. Under **Presets**, click to select **Left** or **Right** option (depending on your preferences) to create two unequal columns.

4. In case you want more than two columns, feel free to increase the number in the **Number of Columns** box.

5. If necessary, adjust the dimensions in the **Width** and **Spacing** sections for each column, and then click **Ok.**

Remove, Increase, or Decrease Column(s)

Steps

1. Select **the text** of the column(s) you want to remove.

2. Choose **Format → Columns** and under **Presets** click **One** to remove columns

3. Under **Presets** click **Two** to increase. Or use the box next to **Number of Columns** to increase or decrease, or

4. Click **Columns** on the **Standard** toolbar and simply select one column to decrease.

Formatting

Find and Replace

The Find and Replace feature is one of the most important features of Microsoft Word. It enables you to search for and optionally replace a specific text or styles with another text or style. For example: Lets assume you would like to find the word "Clinician" and replace it with "Psychiatrist," All you need to do is follow the simple steps outlined below:

Steps

1. Choose **Edit** → **Replace** (or press **Ctrl + H**) to open the **Find and Replace** dialog window:

2. Click to place the cursor in the **Find What** text box, and type the word you want to find and replace.

3. Use the **Tab** key on your key board to move to the **Replace With** text box, and type the word you want to replace with.

4. Click the **Find Next** button to begin the search.

5. When the first occurrence is found, you can choose to **Replace** the first occurrence only or **Replace all**.

6. When you're finished, click the **Close** or **Cancel** button (depending on your version of Word) to close the **Find and Replace** dialog window.

Notepad

While in the Find and Replace dialog window, feel free to experiment with the More>> button to some of the options available such replacing special characters or defining what exactly to search and replace.

Paragraph Spacing

It is easier to customize the paragraph spacing in Microsoft Word for the exact spacing of your choice either between paragraphs or between the lines in a specified paragraph.

Steps

1. Mover the cursor anywhere in the paragraph to be modified, or highlight (select) the entire paragraph.

   Choose **Format** → **Paragraph** to display the following dialog window:

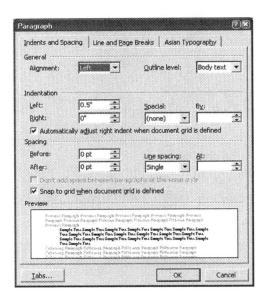

2. Click the **Indents and Spacing** tab if not already active.

3. Under **Spacing,** select **Before** and **After** to increase or decrease by points the number of lines before or after a paragraph (6 points = 1 line). However, my advice to you is to leave the **Before** and **After** at zero (0) unless you really have to change it, and then

4. Click the **drop-down arrow** under **Line Spacing** to choose from **Single** or **1.5 lines, Double,** or **At least,** or **Exactly,** or **Multiple.**

5. If you choose **At least,** or **Exactly** or **Multiple** options, you will have to enter a number in the **At** text box.

6. Click **Ok** when you finish.

Notepad

If you are not happy with the choices made, you can always use the **Undo** button or **Ctrl + Z** to return your document or paragraph to the way it was before changes were made.

Long Documents and Bookmarks

As you have read on page 36, working on a long document can sometimes require that you stop to do something else such as look for more information or simply take a break. Getting back to where you left off can be difficult to remember most especially if you are concerned as to where certain information appears in the document.

To minimize chances of having to go from page to page in search of where you saw whatever it is you are looking for; Microsoft Word makes it possible to navigate your way around easily without having to spend valuable time looking endlessly. One of the things you can do is to use hidden bookmarks. Using hidden bookmarks are very easy to do and you can easily put them anywhere depending on the information you are looking for.

Applying Bookmarks

1. Go to the exact location in your document where you want to place a bookmark and click.

2. Choose **Insert → Bookmark.** And when the following dialog window pops up

3. Type any name for your bookmark in the **Bookmark name,** and then

4. Click **Add.**

Using Bookmark to find a location

1. Press **F5** to open the **Find and Replace** dialog window.

2. Click the **Go To** tab.

3. You don't have to necessarily click **Bookmark** under **Go To What.** All you need to do is simply type the bookmark name in the field under **Enter page number.**

4. Click "**Go To**" to get to the information you bookmarked.

Add Watermarks to personalize your documents

Watermarks are good for indisputable authenticity. It is simply a text (usually a one word text or phrase) that appear behind the main text. You can also use picture, graphic or logo as watermark within your text. You can use it to identify the document's source or status of a document. Adding a watermark to a document is now easier than ever.

To add a watermark

1. Choose **Insert → Picture → WordArt** and when the following windows pops up

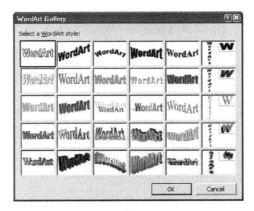

2. Click second column of the first row, and click **Ok.** That should lead you to the *Edit WordArt Text* screen.

3. Type the text you want to use as watermark, and click **Ok.**

4. If the text you just typed appears over your text don't panic. All you have to do is click on it (the WordArt text you just inserted).

5. Choose **Format → WordArt** and from the following window:

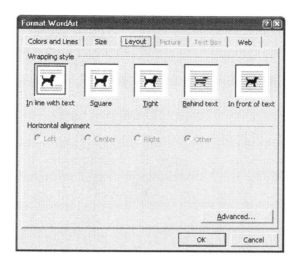

6. Click on the **Layout** tab and then click on the image in the **Behind text** box.

7. Click the **Colors and Lines** tab and under **Fill,** click in the field next to **Color** and on the color palette, select **Light Green.**

8. Under **Line,** click in the field next to **Color** and select **White.**

9. Click **Ok.** If the watermark is not well positioned, you can always click on it and drag to the location of choice to you.

Another way to insert watermark is to:

1. Choose **Format → Background,** and then click **Printed Watermark.**

2. "To insert a picture as a watermark, click **Picture watermark,** and then click **Select Picture.** Select the picture you want, and then click **Insert."**

3. "To insert a text watermark, click **Text watermark,** and then select or enter the text you want."

4. "Select any additional options you want, and then click **Apply."**

5. "To view a watermark as it will appear on the printed page, click **Print Layout** on the **View** menu."

Notepad

This last option may prove to be too difficult and almost impossible to see your watermark. To preview the watermark, click **View → Print Layout**, or, Click **File → Print Preview**, or wait until you print a hard copy of your document. However, I strongly recommend the first option.

Headers and Footers

At times there is a need to create simple headers and footers with just company's name and address (letter head), or complex headers and footers that include company logo, document number, the name of the author, or any relevant information.

Formatting headers and footers are basically the same as formatting any part of your document. The only difference is that they are positioned at the top and bottom margins of each page with the default setting of 0.5"

Creating headers and footers

1. Choose **View → Header and Footer** to display the following **Header** pane (along with its floating toolbar).

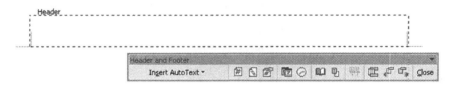

2. Type whatever information for your header, and to create a footer.

3. Click the **Switch Between Header and Footer** which is the third button to the left of **Close** on the floating **Header and Footer** toolbar.

4. To include **Page Number**, click the first button to the right of **Insert AutoText**. Next is the **Number of Pages**, followed by current **Date or Time**, and when you finish with the **Header and Footer** toolbar.

5. Click **Close** on the floating toolbar to return to your document.

Notepad

When you are creating header or footer, use the **Insert AutoText** button on the **Header and Footer** floating toolbar to insert common entries such as the file name and page X of Y (total number of pages).

Inserting Page Numbers outside of Header and Footer

To make your long documents easier to read and reference, you need to insert page numbers. When you insert page number Word automatically formats them in the header or footer section of each document. You can then use the same techniques for working with headers and footers to format page numbers. Follow these steps to insert page numbers:

1. While in Normal view or Page Layout view (Print Layout View), choose **Insert → Page Numbers** to display the following dialog window.

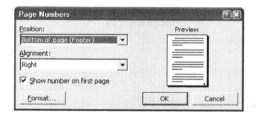

2. From the **Position** list box, click to select one of the available two options: **Bottom of Page (Footer)**, or **Top of Page (Header)**.

3. From the **Alignment** list box, click to select where to place numbers on each page **Left**, or **Center**, or **Right**, or **Inside**, or **Outside**.

4. If you want to start page numbering from the first page, you've got to place a check mark in the box next to **Show Number on First Page**

5. There are still more selections you can make base on your preferences. Click the **Format** button and that should take you to the following **Page Number Format** dialog window.

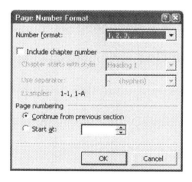

6. From this window, feel free to format page number as your document demand and after that,

7. Click **Ok** to return to the **Page Numbers** dialog window,

8. Click **Ok** or **Close** to return to the document page.

"The music is nothing if the audience is deaf."

Walter Lippmann

Chapter Eleven

Document Layout and Printing

Objectives

When you finish this chapter, you will be able to:

- Create and compile index
- Create forms
- Insert clip art, wrap text, and word count
- Print document

You may have noticed that this section seems to be the longest of them all. Bear with me just a little while longer. We only have a few more important topics to go over and I can't wait to finish. My little girl called and she's already looking forward to "Liz McGuire the Movie" with Hillary Duff. A little while ago it was "Like Mike" with Bow Wow. When are all these going to end? Anyway, let's hurry up and finish this section and the next one. Ok?

Creating Index

If you are creating a long document with so many pages and topics, you will find the use of **Index** very helpful. Index provides the page numbers where you can find whatever topic(s) you are looking for. "Without an index, readers will have difficulty locating information in long documents."

There are three steps to creating index. First of all, you must identify each entry you want to index. Next, you have to collect the marked entries into an index and the last step is to compile your index. Follow the steps outlined below to create index for your "Employee Handbook," "Business Description and Policy," and any other large document you are likely to deal with.

1. Highlight (select) the word or phrase you want to index (one word or one phrase at a time).

2. Choose **Insert**, → **Index and Tables** (if you are using Word XP, choose **Insert** → **Reference** → **Index and Tables**) to display the following dialog window.

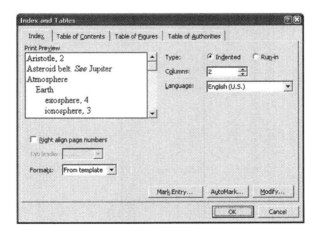

3. Click the **Index** tab (if not already displayed) to display available indexing options.

4. Choose the **Mark Entry** button to display the following **Mark Index Entry** dialog window.

5. You should see the word or phrase you selected in Step 1 displayed in the **Main Entry** text box. To make changes to any of the texts, click in the text box to make your changes.

6. Under **Options,** click any of the radio buttons to select one of the index entry options—**Cross-Reference**, or **Current Page**, or **Page Range Bookmark**, and then choose the **Mark** button. Notice that the dialog window stays open so you can mark multiple entries.

7. Click outside of the dialog window (without closing it) to select the next word or phrase you want to mark, and when you finish, click on the dialog window and then repeat step 6 above. Again, the new word or phrase will be displayed in the **Main Entry** text box; choose **Mark** and repeat until all entries are marked.

8. When you finish marking all entries, click **Close**.

Compiling Index

The next action is to compile those entries into a list, usually in the back (the last page) of the document you just indexed. Follow these steps to compile your document:

1. Go to the location where you would like the index to appear and click to place the cursor at the beginning of that location. If any non-printing character including field codes is displayed, turn it off.

2. Choose **Insert** → **Index and Tables** to display the dialog window.

3. Choose the **Index** tab if it is not already active.

4. Click to select either of the radio buttons next to **Indented** or **Run-In** to indicate the type of index you want to build (as you select, watch the **Print Preview** section reacting to whichever button you click).

5. In the **Formats** list box, select from one of the several choices available, and watch the **Print Preview** area as it displays an example of what the index will look like base on your choice.

6. If you want the index in more than two columns, change the number in the **Columns** spin box.

7. In the **Tab Leader** drop-down list box, click to select the leader *style* you want to use.

8. Click **Ok** to compile the index.

Creating Forms

Forms are a valuable tool in any office environment. It is one of many ways to get people to interact thereby lighting the load of Administrative staff. Forms (soft forms such as Web forms or hard copy such as printed forms) are used to collect information. However, until a few years ago, creating forms (most especially web forms) was almost impossible for an average person. There was a time you think you needed a programming degree just to create forms. Thanks to advancement in technology, you can now do it without having to make anybody miserable.

Whether you are designing a soft form (for use in a Web page) or a hard copy form (printed form), the elements required to design a form are basically the same. "Typically, forms you created are saved as templates so they can be used repeatedly. When filled out and saved, the template remains as you originally created it. Forms can be part of a document or an independent document. They may be short or several pages long." To design a form, follow these steps:

1. Choose **View** → **Toolbars** → **Forms** and move the form toolbar to a convenient place in the toolbar area on your Word screen.

2. Choose **File** → **New** to start a new document or, if you are going to insert the form in an existing document, click to place your cursor in the particular area where you want to begin designing your form.

3. Type the label for the first form field. On the **Forms** toolbar, click **Text Form Field** [abl]. Double-click the field to specify a default entry so that the user does not have to type an entry except to change the response.

4. On the **Forms** toolbar, click **Check Box Form Field** [✓]. You can also use this button to insert a check box next to each item in a group of choices that are not mutually exclusive—that is, users can select more than one.

5. On the **Forms** toolbar, click **Drop-Down Form Field** [▦].

6. Double-click the drop-down form field. To add an item, type the name of the item in the **Drop-down item** box, and then click **Add**.

7. To remove or change the order of item in a drop down-field list form field, Double-click the drop-down form field you want to change.

8. Do any of the following, and then click **OK**:

    a. To delete an item, click the item in the **Items in drop-down list** box, and then click **Remove**.

    b. To move an item, click the item in the **Items in drop-down list** box, and then click the **Move** arrow buttons.

9. Change the formatting of form field result, Select the form field you want to format.

10. On the **Format** menu, click **Font**.

11. Select the options you want.

12. Display or remove shading, Click **Form Field Shading** [a] on the **Forms** toolbar.

13. Add Help or automation to the form. Do any of the following:

    a. Double-click the form field to which you want to add Help text.

    b. Click **Add Help Text**.

    c. To display Help text in the status bar, click the **Status Bar** tab, click **Type your own**, and then type your Help text in the box.

To display Help text in a message box when a user presses F1, click the **Help Key (F1)** tab, click **Type your own**, and then type your Help text in the box.

14. Save the form as a template or as a Word document either way, you will be able to print it out.

15. If you are creating a Web form, and you want to protect the form with a password, click the **Protect Form** button in the **Forms** toolbar.

16. To include a password, choose **Tools → Protect Document** to open the following dialog window:

17. Click **Forms** and then enter a password. Click **Ok** and that should activate **Confirm Password** dialog window, re-enter the exact same password and click **Ok**.

18. Add protection to test a form as you design or change it—On the Forms toolbar, click **Protect Form** 🔒 . You can manually reset form fields by clicking **Reset Form Fields** ✏️ on the **Forms** toolbar.

19. Add protection to help prevent users from changing a form

    1. On the **Tools** menu, click **Protect Document**.

    2. In the **Protect Document** task pane, under **Editing restrictions**, select the **Allow only this type of editing in the document** check box, and then click **Filling in forms** in the list of editing restrictions.

    3. To add protection to only parts of a form, click **Select sections**, and then clear the check boxes for the sections you don't want to add protection to.

4. Click **Yes, Start Enforcing Protection**.

5. To assign a password to the form so that users who know the password can remove the protection and change the form, type a password in the **Enter new password (optional)** box, and then confirm the password. Users who don't know the password can still enter information in the form fields.

20. Save the form, and then distribute it as you would any other document that you send for review.

Notepad

To automate your form, create appropriate macro or if you find the right macro in another template, do not hesitate to copy them into your form template. My recommendation is that you use macros from trusted sources only. Use caution when you are adding macros to your form. Log on to www.mednetservices.com for more information on forms and macros.

Dealing with Graphics

At times you need to insert business logo, pictures, clip art, drawings, and in the case of Web pages you may need to include movies, sound and music. This group of possibilities is known as Graphics. However, dealing with them in Microsoft Word is relatively easy to do. In a way, Word graphics such as drawings, picture, and clipart or business logo remains float on the page and text can be designed to flow around them or simply remain as a stand alone object. Floating makes it possible to drag the graphic from one location to a new place in the document. For an in-depth discussion of graphics, visit www.mednetservices.com

Inserting Clip Art

Inserting *clip art* and picture provides an easy way to add visual appeal to a document. Locating any of the images included in *Microsoft Word* is relatively easy. However, *Word XP (2002)* is designed to rearrange clip arts and other images in your system a little differently. More about that at www.mednetservices.com To insert Clip Art, carefully follow these steps:

1. Click to place the cursor at the exact location in the document where you want the image to appear.

2. Choose **Insert**, → **Picture**, → **Clip Art** to open the *Word 2000* Clip Art Gallery dialog window:

3. Click on the **Clip Art** tab to activate it (if not already activated).

4. Scroll through the categories and when you find a category of interest to you, click on the category and choose from the available Images in that category.

Notepad

As you will discover, nearly all the different versions of Word currently available handles the issue of **Inserting Clip Art** differently. With Word 2000, you have the option to create new category and then import picture into the new category. However, in Word XP, you can have the program **Collect** every available **Clip Arts** in your system automatically. For more information, visit www.mednetservices.com

Wrapping Text

You can wrap text around almost any object—clip arts, business logo, picture, charts and even boxes. This is also known as controlling text flow. Take a careful look at the following real Newspaper Ad and you will see how the text flows around the object (a book entitled "Shrouded in Mystery"). To control text flow around any image, follow the steps outlined below:

Volume One of "Beyond Cut, Copy and Paste." By Dr. Henry Balogun

This volume covers step-by-step explanation of mail merge using Microsoft Word 97 and 2000. It is available at nearly all online bookstores and some local bookstores. Now is the time to start doing more than just Cut, Copy and Paste. Some of the local places you are likely to find a copy include Barnes and Noble Booksellers. You can also obtain a copy through any of the following online booksellers: www.amazon.com or www.walmart.com or www.bn.com

Steps (Word 2000 and Word XP–2002)

1. Click on the image to be sure you have the focus of the system on the image itself.

2. Choose **Format** → **Picture**. When the **Format Picture** window pops up

3. Click the **Layout** tab, and then click any of the available images which indicate how the system will wrap text around the object. Available choices are: **In line with text** or **Square** or **Tight** or **Behind text** or **In front of text.**

4. You can also choose how to position the object within your text. Under **Horizontal Alignment** feel free to choose between; **Left** or **Center** or **Right** or **Other.**

Word Count

When it comes to document handling, setting limitation is not uncommon nowadays. Your project director may ask you to produce 2500 words or less. Perhaps you are responding to a Web request asking you not to exceed 500 words. Hey, lets face it, its not like you don't know how to count but when you know that the phone is going to ring in a few seconds or somebody is going to interrupt your concentration very shortly, why would you want to take on such a head spinning task anyway! If you are really looking for challenges, you are better off running with the bulls in Spain. But as far as word count is concerned, let your Microsoft Word do the counting for you. But don't blame me if you go over the requirement of your project and every idea look so great you don't know which one to delete. To keep track, follow this steps:

1. From Word 2000, click **File** → **Properties** and you should see the following pop up Window:

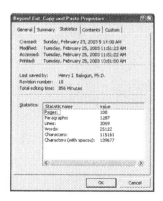

2. Click the **Statistics** tab and the **Statistics** window should display among other things, the number of words you have so far.

3. Click **Ok.**

4. From *Word XP-2002*, choose **Tools** → **Word Count** to count and recount as required

5. To use the new **Word Count** toolbar available only in Word XP, on the **View** menu, point to **Toolbars** and click **Word Count.** This should display the **Word Count** Toolbar at the bottom right corner in the toolbar area of your screen.

6. Then click **Recount** to update the count any time you want. You can also choose to see the current number of **characters**, **lines**, **pages**, and **paragraphs**.

Printing

Needless to say, we've covered a lot of interesting and useful topics and there is no better time to produce an excellent hard copy.

After you have previewed your document, you can send the document directly to a printer, thereby print the current page, a group of pages (page range), or the whole document. You can even compress a document to print two or more pages on one sheet of paper to avoid wasting papers during preview and proofreading.

Your document is not the only thing you can print in Microsoft Office. You can print pictures or any image. If you have created AutoText entries, like we did earlier, you may find it useful to print the list for reference. Not only that, If you have inserted comments in your document (like the feedback we received from the Clinical Director) to provide a note to yourself or other readers (in case you are a team member working on one large document), you may also find it useful to print those comments. I'm going to guide you as to how to print any of the following:

AutoText Entries, Comments and Key Assignments

Steps

1. You can print AutoText entries from any document window. Go to **File** → **Print** to display the following Print dialog window.

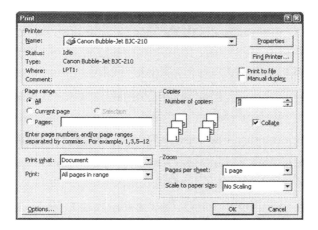

2. Click the option box next to **Print What**, and select **AutoText entries**.

3. Click **Ok** and you should see your *AutoText entry* prints with the abbreviation in bold on one line and the *AutoText entry* on another line.

4. To print **Comments** or **Key Assignments**, repeat step 3 but instead of AutoText entries, select **Comments** or **Key Assignments** and after that

5. Click **Ok**.

Documents Printing

If you are quickly going to print the entire document to the default printer, you may find that the **Print** button on the **Standard** toolbar is a lot faster to use. Word would not display the Print dialog window. However, if you are concerned about changing print options, the Print dialog window is no doubt, your best bet.

Steps

1. Choose **File** → **Print** to display the Print dialog window shown on the previous page.

2. Click the drop down option box next to the **Name** list box, and select the drop-down arrow.

3. Choose a printer. If you are on a network and have shared network printers installed, you will see it listed.

4. Click the **Properties** button to display available options for the currently selected printer.

5. Make appropriate changes with regard to **Paper, Graphics, Fonts,** and **Device Options** tabs—both the tabs and options may differ depending on the printer type.

6. Click **Ok** to return to the **Print** dialog window.

7. To print one copy of the whole document, leave the other options as they are and choose **Ok.**

8. To print more than one copy, feel free to adjust the **Number of Copies**

9. To **Collate,** click to put a check mark in the option box next to **Collate.** This will print one set of the same document at a time.

10. To print page range, under **Page Range** select **All** to print the entire document, or **Current Page** to print the page where cursor is located or blinking, or select **Pages** and type the page ranges you want to print. In Word you are not limited in how you can define your page range. For example: you can choose to print pages **22–28** (avoid using the word "to." To print pages 1, 8, and 18, you would type **1,8,18** (no space). Also, Word allows you to even mix range definitions; such as **1,8,18,22-28.**

11. Once you finish making changes, click **Ok** to start printing.

Printing two pages of text on one sheet of paper

We have to proofread what we have done so far to make corrections if we have to. But one thing we cannot afford right now is to waste papers and ink. Don't forget that part of the overall goal of this clinic is to minimize cost and maximize profit. We don't want our effort to result in wasteful spending. Fortunately for us, Microsoft Word 2000 and XP have a variety of ways to achieve this objective.

You can save paper by printing your document on both sides of the paper even if your printer does not support printing on both sides. Regardless, I'm going to show you how to do this without going over your budget.

1. Choose **File → Print.**

2. From the **Print** window under **Zoom** you can select two or more pages of a document to print on a single sheet of paper. One quick note: any action taken here will not change or affect the formatting and page layout of your document.

3. Click **Ok.**

Notepad

Please bear in mind that when you print more than two pages of text on each sheet of paper, it is highly likely that you will not be able to read your document without the help of a magnifying glass. In that wise, I strongly recommend you limit the number of pages per sheet of paper to two in order to make it readable. But if you are not going to use this feature to proofread your document, and you are not seriously concerned about its readability but just its layout, then you can increase to any number of pages to be printed on a sheet of paper. But keep it simple.

"A real friend is one who walks in when the rest of the world walks out."

Walter Winchell

Chapter Twelve

Integration within Microsoft Office

Objectives

When you finish this chapter, you will be able to:

- Embed Excel Worksheets in Word
- Copy an Excel table in Word
- Insert PowerPoint presentation in Word

The inability of one program to perform what other programs can do so very well is not really of a serious concern in Microsoft Office. You are well aware that there are some calculations you can perform in Microsoft Word table but on the other hand, there are a lot you wouldn't be able to do. However, if you are having problems doing those calculations in Word, you can simply walk across the isle (not literally) and bring Excel into Word and this is known as embedding. When you embed Excel worksheet into Word, you are in a way asking Excel to come into the Word suite with all its worksheets, formulas, menus and toolbars.

In this section, we are going to deal extensively with embedding Excel worksheets in Word Documents. This will lead us to do some of the complex calculations we would love to do in Word but could not do due to its limitations. The **Insert Microsoft Excel Worksheet** button on the **Standard** toolbar lets you embed Excel worksheet in Word document.

We've just been asked to send a memo to every Psychiatrist and Therapist including Case Managers to let them know that the Central Office is in the process of closing some cases. The closing is scheduled to affect patients who have not been back in the clinic within the last 60 days for whatever reasons. But before this closing, we have to inform each Psychiatrist, Therapist and Case Manager just in case they would like to contact any of those patients to inform them about the pending action of the central office.

Create a Memorandum

Regardless of which style you prefer, all memorandum styles contain, basically, the same elements. The lead words area is usually in double space and with the following elements:

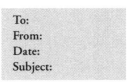

To:
From:
Date:
Subject:

The body of the memo comes next and is usually in single space. The last part of the memo could be a Reference, or an Attachment. To fully understand this, let us reproduce the following memo:

MidMed©

To:	Psychiatrists and Therapists
From:	Clinical Director
Date:	February 17, 2005
Subject:	Administrative Discharge

Our record indicates that the following patients have been in inactive status for more than 60 days and we are about to initiate administrative discharge. I'm hereby asking you to carefully review the following list and kindly contact those that are your patients to inform them of the pending action.

cc: Vice President of Operations

Embedding Excel Worksheets in Word

1. Click to place the cursor at the location where you want to insert Excel Worksheet. In our case, we are going to insert the worksheet after the last line of the only paragraph in the Memo. At the end of "inform them of the pending action," press **Enter**.

2. Click **Insert Microsoft Excel Worksheet** button on the **Standard** toolbar.

3. Move your mouse to cover all the rows and columns and click the mouse. Expand the worksheet to accommodate five rows and six columns

4. Enter the following information:

   a. First row, **Column one** = Patient ID, **Column two** = First Name, **Column three** = Last Name, **Column four** = SS Number, **Column five** = Admission Date and **Column six** = Phone Number. Feel free to format the heading as you like.

   b. In column one of the second row, type the following formula (no space anywhere):

   =Left(B2)&Left(C2)&Right(D2,4) and press **Enter**

5. Choose **Data → Form**, and

   a. Enter the following information (without comma) beginning from the first active field: First Name = **Avon,** Last Name = **Lady,** SS

Number = **021-34-9191**, Admission Date = **12/25/2002**, and Phone Number = **215-555-1212**

b. Click **New** and enter the following two patients information (don't forget to click **New** again to enter the next information):

First Name: Sugar	Flowing
Last Name: Daddy	Alien
SS Number: 321-45-9494	645-34-9595
Admission Date: 01/21/2003	01/24/2003
Phone Number: 717-555-1212	610-555-1212

c. Click **Close.**

6. Click **outside** of the Excel Worksheet to return to the Word mode.

When you have finished, your memo should look like this:

MidMed©

To:	Psychiatrists and Therapists
From:	Clinical Director
Date:	February 17, 2005
Subject:	Administrative Discharge

Our record indicates that the following patients have been in inactive status for more than 60 days and we are about to initiate administrative discharge. I'm hereby asking you to carefully review the following list and kindly contact those that are your patients to inform them of the pending action.

Patient ID	First Name	Last Name	SS Number	Admission Date	Phone Number
AL9191	Avon	Lady	021-34-9191	12/25/2002	215-555-1212
SD9393	Sugar	Daddy	025-51-9393	12/26/2002	610-555-1212
FA9595	Flowing	Alien	645-34-9595	1/24/2003	610-555-1212

cc: Vice President of Operations

Copy an Excel Table in Word

Another way to handle the task we just finished is to complete the worksheet in Excel and copy it into Word document. The feature for this also provides the option to have Excel retain its formatting, and also match the table style in Excel with the copy in Word document. Not only that, changes made to the original will also reflect in the copy. Unfortunately, this feature is only available in Excel XP (2002). Follow the steps outlined below to copy a table from Excel to Word:

1. Open Excel, and select the table you want to copy.

2. On the **Edit** menu, click **Copy**, or right-click on the selected table and on the pop up menu, click **Copy**

3. Open **Microsoft Word** without closing Excel, and then click where you want to insert the table.

4. Click **Edit** and then click **Paste Options**.

5. To link the table so that it automatically updates when changes are made in the source (the original Excel copy), select **Keep Source Formatting and Link to Excel**, and otherwise select **Keep Source Formatting**.

Insert PowerPoint Presentation in Word

You can include a PowerPoint presentation in a Word document. It also provides the option to have PowerPoint retain its formatting, and also match the presentation style in PowerPoint with the copy in Word document. Again, changes made to the original will also reflect in the copy. This is a PowerPoint XP (2002) feature and not available in Word 2000. Follow the steps outlined below to copy a presentation from PowerPoint to Word:

1. Click the area in your Word document where you want the PowerPoint presentation to appear.

2. Choose **Insert** → **Object** to open the following **Object** dialog window.

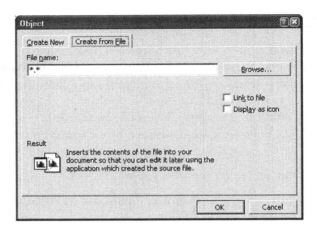

3. Click to activate **Create from File** tab.

4. To link the original presentation in PowerPoint to a Word document, click the check box next to **Link to File**.

5. Click **Browse** to locate the presentation file, and the system should immediately bring you to **Browse** window.

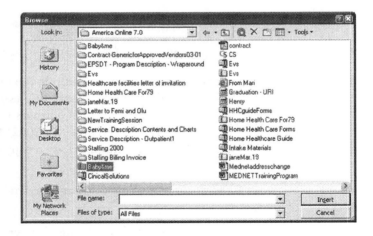

6. Locate and click the appropriate PowerPoint presentation file and click **Insert**.

7. You will see the first of the presentation showing in your Word document.

8. To play the presentation, **double-click** the slide in the Word document, sit back and enjoy.

You will find more explanation on this and some other incredible features available in Microsoft Excel, coming up in the next section.

Microsoft Excel

Here we are going to focus on *Microsoft Excel* exclusively. We are going to take a careful look at the features of this powerful and extremely useful business tool. We are going to take a deeper look at how *Excel* works with the rest of *Microsoft Office* programs.

"Good manners will open doors that the best education cannot."

Clarence Thomas

Chapter Thirteen

Introduction to Excel

Objectives

When this chapter is finish, you will be able to:

- Enter data in Excel
- Select cells and align texts

To fully understand computer applications, programming, or the whole process of the digital divide is to understand its concept. How many times have you heard somebody say, "You have no idea what in the universe I'm talking about, do you?" No matter how hard we try to do something, whatever it is, without proper understanding of its concept, we will always come short, time and again. Understanding concept can sometimes depend on how well rooted and grounded you are in comprehension. To fully comprehend, it is necessary to eliminate any preexisting thought that's likely to interfere with concentration—try as much as possible to avoid a divided attention.

> A tour bus load full of noisy tourists arrives at Runnymede, England.
> They gather around the guide who says, "This is the spot where the barons forced King John to sign the Magna Carta."
> A man pushing his way to the front of the crowd asks, "When did that happen?"
> "1215," answers the guide.
> The man looks at his wristwatch and says, "Shoot! Just missed it by a half hour!"

Microsoft Excel is a program popularly known as an electronic spreadsheet designed to make working with numbers (regardless of whether you are actually comfortable working with numbers or not) something to really enjoy and not something to despise. There is simply no better electronic spreadsheet, or worksheet, as some people like to refer to it.

One of the goals I hope to achieve in this volume is to remove the fear of working with numbers. To make this goal a reality, *Unlock Microsoft Excel* is hereby presented in easy to understand process. You will find how best to work with *Microsoft Excel* and produce the expected result. However, there are so many actions (as you will soon discover) that cannot be performed through point and click without the use of computer instructions, otherwise known as programming, that are capable of repeating themselves until every necessary, important, and required step is completely executed.

Chapter one entitled *Optional Configuration* is written to help you deal with some computer features that are likely to interfere with the use of your computer system. This type of help with basic configuration of the system as opposed to our subject matter, is something you will find in every volume of *Microsoft Office for Healthcare Professionals.* The beginning chapter is always about necessary fine-tuning of your computer system.

Before we begin to unlock *Microsoft Excel*, I'm going to take this time to introduce you to some of Excel features that may have appeared difficult to understand until now. As we go on, you will come across some similarities to *Microsoft Word* (as revealed in Volume one of *Microsoft Office for Healthcare Professionals)* and other members of the *Microsoft Office* group of programs. I will also call your attention to where Excel deviates from those similarities.

Entering Data in Excel

The focus of Excel is usually in the active cell and the active cell is one with the

insertion block otherwise known as the highlight. When Excel is started, the active cell (where you will find the insertion block) is normally at the intersection of row one and column one (**A1**). You can start entering data the moment Excel is started. You can enter text as label in cases where descriptive heading is required, or use specially defined labels such as alphanumeric label. You can also enter numbers, which can be calculated using formulas. Excel is designed to recognize the type of data you enter—text, number, or formula.

Text

Excel does not treat long text the same way as *Microsoft Word*. If a text entry is too long and the cell to the right of the long text is empty, Excel continues and displays the rest of the text over the adjacent cell. But if the cell to the right of the long text contains an entry (number, text, or formula), then Excel limits the text entry to the active cell but truncate the display of the long text. To see the rest of the text, you will have to expand the active cell.

Undo, Redo and Repeat

Even though most actions can be undone, the real deal is that Excel can only reverse your last 16 actions, regardless of whether they are simple or complex. As you have seen in *Microsoft Word*, the **Redo** button reverses **Undo**. The **Edit** → **Repeat** lets you repeat your last action. You can use this command to repeat your last action in as many cells as you like.

Number

It is not really required to enter commas, dollar signs. The best way to handle it is to just enter the numbers and later use Excel formatting commands to add commas, dollar signs and whatever formatting is necessary and required. Always type a decimal point if the number you are entering requires one. Always type a negative number entry with a minus sign or enclose it in parenthesis.

Formulas

Formulas are equations that perform calculations on values in your worksheet. A formula starts with an equal sign (=) and does not require the use of space anywhere within the formula. Elements of formulas are as follows:

1. **Operators**. Operator is a sign, or symbol that specifies the type of calculation to perform within an expression.

2. **Constants**. Constant is a value that is not calculated and therefore does not change.

3. **Relative reference**. In a formula, the address of a cell based on the relative position of the cell that contains the formula and the cell referred to.

4. **Name**. A word or string of characters that represents a range of cells, formulas, or constant value.

Selecting Cells

There are some striking similarities to *Microsoft Word* with regard to steps required to select, or highlight texts, or numbers. You can use the mouse or the keyboard to select cells. Once cells are selected or highlighted, you can move, copy, delete or simply format as you like. However, selecting a letter or a word in a long text is not as easy in Excel as it is in Word. And when you try to select or highlight more than one cell, the first cell (the cell you started from) will look like it is on strike—like its not part of the group of cells you are trying to select. Before you start talking to yourself or yelling at your neighbor or pulling out your hair (just kidding!), I want you to know that the first cell is not being difficult or rebellious—that's just the way it is supposed to appear. Nothing is wrong with your computer system or the application you are using. All I can say is welcome to the sometimes wacky world of computer technology.

Aligning

By default, texts are aligned to the left of a cell and numbers to the right of a cell.

You can always use the **Align Left, Center** or **Align Right** buttons on the toolbar to adjust as you like. Again, this is applicable to cells. You can only align within a cell or group of cells but not within an entire page as in Microsoft Word.

Other similarities to *Microsoft Word* are in the layout of their menus and toolbars. Excel menu responds the same way to *Access Keys*. Each underlined letter works with the **Alt** key. Hold down the **Alt** key and then press any of the **Access Keys** (the underlined letter) and it will activate the pull down menu.

Excel toolbars display screen tips just like in Microsoft Word but not along with screen shortcut. To activate screen tips, click **Tools → Customize → Option** and then click the check box next to **Show screen tips on toolbars.**

Finally, you will notice that Excel gives you a blank **workbook** in which there are three **worksheets** to begin with. You are not by any means limited to those three worksheets. You can always add more depending on your need. However, these worksheets are similar to a paper notebook which consists of many pages or sheets of paper.

Unlike a paper notebook, Excel comes with gridlines with horizontal rows and vertical columns. Each worksheet in Excel has 256 columns and 65,536 rows—that's an unbelievably large worksheet. The point where each row and each column meet (intersect) is known as a **cell.** For example, the point where the first row meets the first column or the second column or the third and so on and so forth is known as a **cell.** How many rows and columns are displayed at any given time depend in large measure on the size of your screen. Regardless, you can always scroll right or left, up or down to reach the rest of the rows and columns.

Introduction to this program whose name connotes essence of achievement more than it does of a computer application designed to be a comprehensive business tool could go on and on, instead, let us just stop right here and begin to unfold the beauty of this incredible application.

The last chapter (presented in dialogue format) is designed to prepare you for my next book which is going to be called "*Beyond e-Mails.*" This type of conclusion is something unique to all of my series. It started from Volume One of "*Microsoft Office for Healthcare Professionals.*"

"It is not enough to do your best; you must know what to do, and then do your best."

W. Edwards Deming

Chapter Fourteen

A Quick look at Excel Features

Objectives

When you finish this chapter, you will be able to:

- Open a new workbook
- Identify and describe the functions of the Name box and Formula bar
- Use Formulas and Functions to perform simple calculations
- Edit and mover around in Excel
- Create vertical titles
- Enter more than one line in a cell
- Identify Excel shortcuts
- Save files in Excel

Starting Excel

How you start Excel or any of the programs in *Microsoft Office* depends on whether you want to open a new file or an existing file. In the case of Excel, to open a file, new or existing is to open a workbook. The process is basically the same.

To Open a New Workbook

1. Click the **🏁 Start** button, place your mouse on **Programs**, or **All Programs** (if your system is equipped with *Windows XP*) from the right pane, look for and select **Microsoft Excel**, or

2. Simply look for and click the Excel 🗷 button on the *Microsoft Office Shortcut bar* from the desktop.

That should open Excel and take you to a blank worksheet in a new workbook that looks like the following screenshot from Excel 2002:

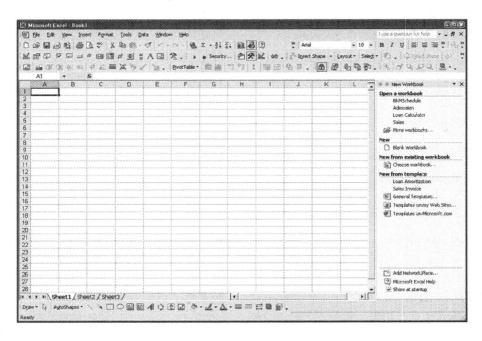

The Insertion block ⬜ is in **A1**. As soon as you start typing, you will see these new toolbar buttons **✕ ✓ ƒx** showing between the **Name** box and the

Formula bar. If you move your mouse on the ✖ button, it should read **Cancel** and the next button ✔ after that should read **Enter.** In Excel, after entering a text, number or formula and you press the **Enter** key on the keyboard, the Insertion block will immediately move down—below the active cell. However, after entering a text, number or formula and you click the **Enter** button on the toolbar, Excel will then perform the required action but keep the **Insertion block** at the same location.

The Name box and Formula Bar

The **Name** box and the **Formula** bar are located on the same line below the toolbars and directly on top of the grid lines and cells. The **Name** box (which is the space directly on top of the "A" column and to the left of the *Formula Bar*) usually displays the address or reference of the active cell. The following screen-shot is taken from Excel 2002, the *Name* box displays "B1" while the *Formula Bar* displays =DATEDIF(A1,TODAY(),"Y")

B1	▼	*fx* =DATEDIF(A1,TODAY(),"Y")					
A	B	C	D	E	F	G	H
1	103						
2							

Apart from displaying cell reference, the *Name* box can be used to:

1. Move to any cell you want. For example, click the **Name** box and type **G27** and then press **Enter.** That should take the **Insertion block** to cell **G27**. This is something you will find useful in a large worksheet.

2. Name a cell or a group of cells (range). Naming cells provides a more efficient way to refer to them when they are needed in formulas, functions, etc. To name a cell or group of cells:

    a. Click the cell you want to name, or select a group of cells (range).

    b. Go to the **Name** box and type the name of the cell or group of cells.

    c. Press the **Enter** key on your keyboard.

3. To jump to a named cell or range of cells:

    a. Click the little arrow next to the Name box and this should display all the cells that are recently named.

b.   Move the mouse over to the name of the cell or range you want to move to and click. Remember, you can only jump to a predefined cell or named cell.

Formula bar and formulas

The **Formula bar** simply displays the contents of the active cell. Formulas are equations that perform calculations on values in your worksheet. A formula starts with an equal sign (=) and should contain no space anywhere. For example, let's use a formula to reveal your age. Yeah, I would like to know how old you are. C'mon we are friends, right? Ok, now use the arrow key on your keyboard to move the **Insertion block** to **B1** and type this formula =**DatedIf(A1,Today(),"Y")**. You've got to type it exactly as it is, no space and do not forget to start with the equal (=) sign. Instead of using the **Enter** key on your keyboard, just click on the **Enter** button. Now take a look at the result. Does the system say you are 103 years old? Wow! Talk about rapid aging, huh? What are you going to do now that you are 103 years old? You are too old for me! Hey, don't come yelling at me, I didn't do it. Why don't you move the **Insertion block** back to **A1** using the left arrow key on your keyboard and tell the system your date of birth by typing it in this format **mm/dd/yyyy** and don't forget to click the **Enter** button, or press the **Enter** key on your keyboard. Does the system say you are 21 years old? Hey, if you are a girl, and perhaps would like to hang out at Seven Eleven or Wawa tonight, give me a call (just kidding!). Now that we both passed the compatibility test, let us examine the role of functions.

Functions

Functions are predefined formulas that perform calculations by using specific values, called arguments, in a particular order, or structure. Functions can be used to perform simple or complex calculations. For example, let us enter the following:

1.   In **A4**, type 9 and press the **Enter** key on your keyboard.

2.   In **A5** type 20 and press the **Enter** key on your keyboard

3.   Repeat the same for the following cells **A6** = 16, **A7** = 14 and **A8** = 23

For the result, move the **Insertion block** to any empty cell of your choice and type the following:

1. **=MIN(A4:A8)** this should give you the smallest number in the range which is 9

2. **=MAX(A4:A8)** this should give you the largest number in the range which in our example, is = 23

3. **=SMALL(A4:A8, 2)** however, this will produce the second smallest number in the range, or 14

4. **=LARGE(A4:A8,3)** on the other hand, this will produce the third largest number in the range, or 16

5. **=AVERAGE(A4:A8)** the system should give you the average of all the numbers entered so far, or 16.40

6. **=SUM(A4:A8)** with this formula, the system should produce the total sum of your numbers.

To view the list of predefined functions currently available in your Microsoft Excel, hold down the **Shift** key and press **F3.** This simple action will take you to a **Paste Function** window—Excel 2000 or **Insert Function** window—Excel 2002. The following is taken from Excel 2002.

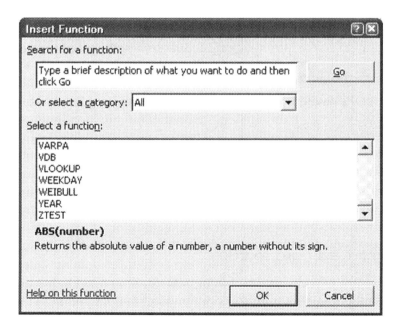

If you are using Excel 2000, under **Function category,** click **All** (in Excel 2002, you will find **All** in the box next to **Or select a category**) and that should lead to a long list of all available **Functions** showing under **Function name.** When you click on any of the functions, you should see explanation of the function showing at the bottom of the window.

Editing in Excel

Ok, you made a mistake in entering text, number or formula, right? To err is human. So my friend, welcome to the human family. You are going to move the **Insertion block** over to the cell to be edited but try not to press any key on the keyboard. As soon as you hit any key, the content of the cell will immediately be replaced. But before I show you how to correct the mistake using your keyboard, let's look at how you can edit using your mouse.

1. Click the **Cell** where the mistake appears and this should display the cell entry in the **Formula bar** ▾ ✕ ✓ *ƒx*

2. Move the **Mouse pointer** to the Formula bar where the cell entry appears and click, and this should activate the cursor.

3. Use the left ⬅ arrow key on your keyboard or the right ⮕ arrow key to move the cursor to where your mistake is and press **Backspace** to erase each character to the left of the cursor, or

4. Press the **Delete** key to erase each character to the right of the cursor, or

5. Use the mouse to select (highlight) characters and type a replacement.

6. When you finish,

    a. Click the **Enter** button on the **Formula bar** or press the **Enter** key to accept the changes, or

    b. Click the **Cancel** button on the **Formula bar** or press the **Esc** key to abort the changes.

Using the Keyboard to Edit

As stated in the previous section, editing with the mouse can sometimes prove difficult and almost impossible to do without deleting the content of a cell or group of cells. Here is a better and more efficient way to edit the content of a cell or group of cells, even hyperlink without using the mouse.

1. Use the **arrow keys** to select (highlight) the cell you want to edit.

2. Press **F2** to edit the cell contents—this action will immediately place the cursor at the end of the cell entry.

3. Use the **Backspace** to delete to the right or use the left **Arrow key** on your keyboard to move to the exact point where you want to edit.

4. When you have finished, just press **Enter** to accept your changes, or press **Esc** to cancel the changes (in case you change your mind).

AutoSum

One common calculation function in Excel is the **Sum** function. The main focus is simply to manipulate all the numbers in a range of cells either by adding them together or looking for minimum, maximum, average and or weighted average. For example let's reproduce the following and carry out the steps enumerated below:

Sales Person	Invoice
Maria	125
Crystal	253
John	350
Ryan	258
Jose	560
Total	1546

1. In **A7** type **Total**

2. Move the **Insertion block** to **B7** and click the **AutoSum** Σ button on the **Standard** toolbar

3. When the formula **=Sum(B2:B6)** appears, press the **Enter** key on your keyboard or click on the **Enter** button on the toolbar to accept it. That should produce a total of **1546**.

Moving around in Excel

To move:

1. To cell A1 from anywhere in your worksheet, press **Ctrl + Home**

2. To the last row and columns containing data, press **Ctrl + End**

3. Within the same row, press **Left** or **Right Arrow** key

4. To a specific cell address or named range using the **Go To** feature, press **Ctrl + G** or simply press **F5**

5. Within the same column, press the **Up** or **Down Arrow** key

6. To the beginning of the current row, press **Home**

7. Up or down one screen at a time, press **Page Up** or **Page Down**

8. Left or right one screen, press **Alt + Page Up** or **Alt + Page Down**

Create Vertical Titles in Excel

Excel provides an easy way to create a vertical heading which runs along the side of a table as opposed to above it. An example of vertical title is hereby highlighted in green:

MidMed Quarterly Report		Financial Report		
		First Qrt	Second Qrt	Third Qurt
	Medication Checks	123,975.00	128,695.00	135,274.00
	Therapy	126,879.00	129,821.00	136,189.00
	Case Management	132,843.00	136,925.00	142,764.00
	Total	383,697.00	395,441.00	414,227.00

To reproduce the above example, follow these steps:

1. Select or highlight the cell where you want to insert vertical heading, otherwise you may have to format each heading one-by-one.

2. Click **Format** → **Cells**, or simply hold down the **Ctrl** key and press **1** (the number One). That will take you to the following dialog window (Excel 2002):

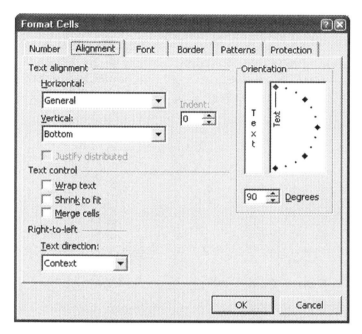

3. Click the **Alignment** tab

4. Increase the **Degrees** text box under *Orientation* to **90**.

5. Select the **Merge cells** text box under *Text Control* and click **OK**.

Notepad

If you are unable to produce the expected "Vertical Titles," you may have to create the vertical title of the heading area cell-by-cell. However, the side vertical can be accomplished by simply placing the insertion block one cell below the "Total" and highlight upward. Example: Let's assume the "Total" is in cell A6, you will have to move the insertion block to **A7**, hold down the **Shift** key and press the **Up Arrow** key until A7 through to A1 is selected and then perform the actions stated in Steps 2–5 above.

Saving Files Automatically in Excel

In real life, if you fail to put your valuables away in a safe place, you might end up losing what is so precious and dear to you. To put all burglars and thieves in your surroundings out of business, you need to develop the habit of making sure your stuff are kept in a safe area before walking away. In Microsoft Excel, it is not unlikely for some unimaginable circumstances to cause you to deviate abruptly from what you are doing, thereby forget to save it. In *Excel 2000*, this type of worry can be dealt with once and for all. *Excel 2000* is fully capable of making sure that all your files are saved before you leave the system. However, the feature that would allow you to enjoy this kind of protection in *Excel 2000* is known as **AutoSave** and it is not installed by default. You will have to install it to use it and here is how:

1. Click **Tools** → and then click **Add-Ins.**

2. Under the **Add-Ins available** list, look for and select the **Autosave Add-in** check box.

3. Click **OK.**

After the Installation, you will have to configure the new feature to use it.

1. Click **Tools** → **AutoSave.**

2. Click to place a check mark next to **Automatic save every.**

3. In the **Minutes** box, enter how often you want Excel to save your workbooks. The default is 10 minutes.

4. If you want the system to let you know before saving, click to place a check mark next to **Prompt Before Saving** box

5. Once you are done, click **OK.**

Moving Between Workbooks or Worksheets in Excel

When you have several workbooks opened with so many worksheets in each workbook, moving around is easier than you think possible. To avoid having to minimize this workbook in order to open that workbook or click on this worksheet and then click on that worksheet, all you have to do is:

1. Press **Ctrl + Tab** to move from one workbook to another workbook,

2. Press **Ctrl + Page Down** to move from one worksheet to another work-sheet (from left to right). To move back from worksheet to worksheet (right to left), press **Ctrl + Page Up.**

Enter More Than One Line in an Excel Cell

It is not impossible to enter more than one line of text in a cell or group of cells in Microsoft Excel. In case you need to enter a line break within a cell, follow this step:

1. Hold down the **Alt** key and press the **Enter** key once. This will enable you to start a new line within the same cell.

However, if you should have the need to wrap text automatically to fit the column width, follow these steps:

2. Click the cell of choice to you.

3. Click **Format → Cells,** and then click the **Alignment** tab

4. Click the check box next to **Wrap text**

5. Click **Ok.**

Data in the cell will wrap to fit the column width. You can make the column wider or narrower to adjust the width of the data.

Excel Shortcuts

Calculate all sheets in all open workbooks	F9
Calculate the active worksheet	SHIFT+F9
Copy	CTRL+C
Create a chart that uses the current range	F11 or ALT+F1
Display the **Format Cells** dialog box	CTRL+1
Display the **Go To** dialog box	F5
Fill the selected cell range with the current entry	CTRL+ENTER
Insert the current time	CTRL+:

Insert today's date	CTRL+;
Move to the beginning of the worksheet	CTRL+HOME
Move to the last cell on the worksheet, which is the cell at the intersection of the rightmost used column and the bottommost used row (in the lower-right corner), or the cell opposite the home cell, which is typically A1	CTRL+END
Open	CTRL+O
Paste	CTRL+V
Paste a function into a formula	SHIFT+F3
Print	CTRL+P
Save	CTRL+S
Select all (when you are not entering or editing a formula)	CTRL+A
Select the current column	CTRL+SPACEBAR
Select the current row	SHIFT+SPACEBAR
Undo	CTRL+Z
When you enter a formula, display the **Formula Palette** after you type a function name	CTRL+A

Exiting Excel

After using Excel or any of the programs/applications in *Microsoft Office* (or any other program for that matter), you should always make the effort to exit the application gracefully. *Microsoft Excel* (like the rest of Office programs) is designed to perform necessary housekeeping before it closes.

If after you click save you decided to modify any of your Excel worksheets and let's assume that changes to the worksheet have not been saved, any attempt to exit will compel Excel to bring out a small pop up window asking the following question:

Do you want to save the changes to "File Name?"

If you want to save all changes, all you need to do is click **Yes** for Excel to save changes to your document before leaving the program, otherwise, click **No**.

"When you are inspired by some great purpose, some extraordinary project, all your thoughts break their bounds: Your mind transcends limitations, your consciousness expands in every direction, and you find yourself in a new, great, and wonderful world. Dormant forces, faculties, and talents become alive, and you discover yourself to be a greater person by far than you ever dreamed yourself to be."

Patanjali

Chapter Fifteen

Managing a Database

Objectives

When you finish this chapter, you will be able to:

- Create a database from the scratch
- Prevent invalid data entry
- Add, modify, and delete records in a database
- Sort database according to predefined criteria

To try and explain a program this complex and highly important business tools known as Excel, I am going to employ the use of surgical database aimed at poking into clinical solutions but designed mainly to educate everyone regardless of your professional affiliation. Once you fully understand the entire concept of Excel as revealed in this book, you will be able to apply the knowledge gained to solve any Excel-related problems. Not only that, you will also be able to use the same knowledge when the time comes to cover Visual Basic for Applications (VBA). Chapter Six which deals with Macro provides a way to start digging into VBA and you will find full explanation of its intricacies in my next book.

We are going to attend to some of the requests from Ms. Jones. In case you are wondering who is Ms. Jones, she is our make believe Clinical Director of MidMed—a relatively big Outpatient Psychiatry. First of all, she is asking us to help her Assistant create a Clinical Solution. This is simply a database that can be used to organize patient information and related information such as psychopharmacological treatment (past and present), psychotherapy as well as reimbursement information.

However, the approach I am going to use here slightly deviates from focusing on clinically oriented issues only. It presents a general overview of Excel—one of the most powerful business tools around. The materials covered here are very useful in any professional environment—private or public, for profit or non-profit. For the sake of better understanding, we are going to make some assumptions. We are going to assume that:

1. This clinic (MidMed) does not like randomly generated patient identification number. The Clinical Director would want us to create a unique Patient ID.

2. It is one of the policies of this clinic not to admit any patient less than 5 years old. A patient has to be ≥ 5 years old.

3. The database must reveal the stated patient age to avoid violation of the policy stated above.

What is a database?

To put simply, a database is a collection of organized records such as library index cards, or phone directory. In a clinical environment, collecting information on patients is without doubt an important process that must be done religiously. We usually start with the basic information such as name, address, phone number and social security number and when we do this per patient, we are in a way creating an individual record.

Excel is all about collecting, analyzing and manipulating data. You can create your own database or use one created by a third party vendor. You might want to create a database to keep track of inventory such as supplies and equipment, patient records, provider information, or employees, including all of the entities responsible for paying for services rendered.

In creating a database, there are so many things you need to take into consideration. If several people are going to be maintaining the database, you might want to:

1. Consult many of your administrative and clinical staff to be sure no necessary and required item is left out. It is not always easy to modify a large database designed for use in a large business environment.

2. You will need to clearly define particular entries such as "state abbreviation," "date," or special numbers like "social security numbers." This is necessary to eliminate errors.

How to create a database

Notepad

Warning! This section is relatively complicated most especially if you are a first time Excel users. It is highly recommended that you read this section in its entirety before attempting to create the database using the steps outlined here. Please try and pay very careful attention to details.

In this database template example, we are going to create surgical database aimed at poking into clinical solutions. The purpose of it is mainly to educate. In real world, when you create patient admission database, you will have to include Insurance information, Appointments, as well as Patient background history including past treatment history and more. But in this case, many necessary and required fields are going to be intentionally omitted. This is what I meant by "surgical database aimed at poking into clinical solutions." It is a database designed only to explain steps necessary and required to create real database.

Using wizard to create database

Even though we are going to use the Template Wizard to create our first database, it is also possible and perhaps time efficient to accomplish the same goal through direct approach and that is by typing directly into the data grid (Excel worksheet). However, I am going to show you both and which one you prefer is entirely up to you. To create the first database using the *Template Wizard*, do the following:

1. Click **Data → Template Wizard.** If this is your first time of using this feature, it is very likely the command will not appear on the **Data** menu.

    a. If you are using *Excel 2000*, click **Tools → Add-Ins** and then select **Template Wizard with Data Tracking,** and click **Ok.** After that, go back to **Data → Template Wizard.**

    b. If you are using *Excel 2002 (Excel XP or 2003)*, you will have to log on to http://office.microsoft.com and then in the **Search for** box, type **Template Wizard for Excel 2002** and click **Go.** That should take you to a page where you can click on a hyperlink with this heading: <u>Creating a Data Entry Form with the Template Wizard in Excel 2002</u> or click on <u>Excel 2002 Add-in: Template Wizard with Data Tracking</u>. Feel free to download the **Add-In.** When you have finished downloading, install it right away.

2. Click **Tools → Add-Ins → Template Wizard with Data Tracking → Ok.**

3. Click **Data → Template Wizard** and the following window should pop up

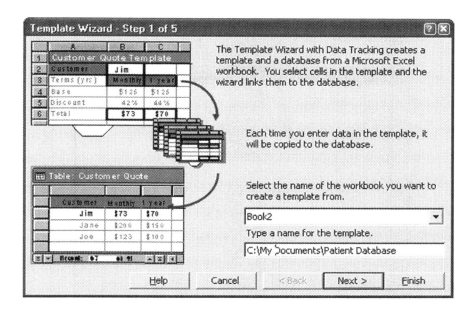

4. In the **Type a name for the template** box, type the following for your data form: *C:\My Documents\Patient Database* and click **Next.** That should take you to the following screen.

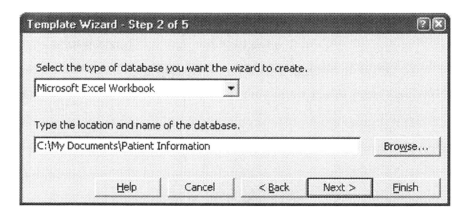

5. In the box next to **Select the type of database you want to create** do not change the default **Microsoft Excel Workbook.** Also in the **Type the location and name of the database,** type the following address: *C:\My Documents\Patient Information*

6. Click **Next** and that should lead you to step 3 of 5 of the **Template Wizard** window:

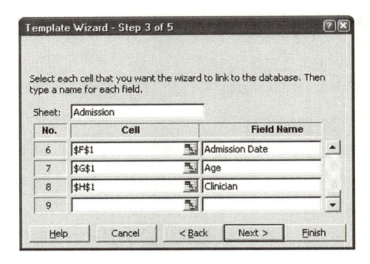

7. In the **Sheet** input box, type *"Admission"* without the quotation marks.

8. In **No. 1 Cell** box, type **$A$1** which is the same as **A1**. By adding the $ sign, you are creating an absolute cell. More explanation of absolute cell later in the next chapter. To avoid typing, click in cell **A1** on the Excel worksheet and that should input **$A$1** in **No. 1 Cell** box automatically.

9. Click back on the **Template Wizard step 3 of 5** window and in the box directly under the **Field Name** type **Patient ID**

10. Click again in cell **B1** of your Excel worksheet and direct across from **No. 2 Cell** under **Field Name** type **First Name**. Enter the following to complete this step:

    a. **No   Cell   Field Name**

    b. 3 $C$1   Last Name

    c. 4 $D$1   SS Number

    d. 5 $E$1   D O B

    e. 6 $F$1   Admission Date

    f. 7 $G$1   Age

    g. 8 $H$1   Clinician

11. After entering the last field name, click **Next** to go the next window (step 4 of 5).

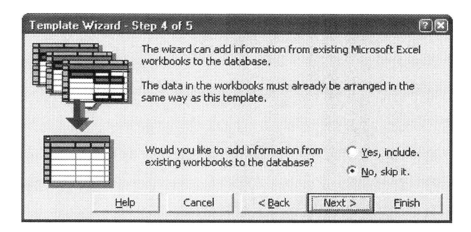

12. From here on, all you need to do is simply click **Next** and that should activate the last window in the **Template Wizard** setup.

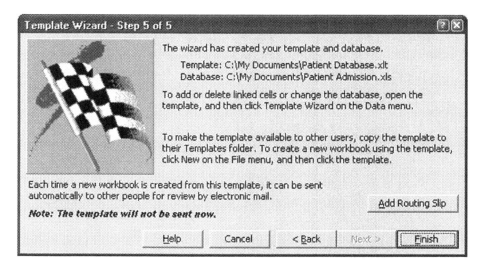

13. Click **Finish** to create your database.

Congratulations, you just created your first database template with the help of the **Template Wizard for Data Tracking.** In some cases your database should appear immediately. But if this does not happen, if your database does not display right away, follow these steps:

1. Click **File → Open**

2. Click the little down arrow next to the **Look in** box and select **Local Disk (C:)**

3. Click **My Documents** directory and when the directory opens, look for an Excel file named; **Patient Information** and click it once to select it.

4. Click **Open** and your Excel worksheet should reveal the following:

	A	B	C	D	E	F	G	H
1	Patient ID	First Name	Last Name	SS Number	D O B	Admission Date	Age	Clinician
2								
3								

Adjust Column Width

As you can see, some of your entries are simply too long for the cell in which they appeared. In Microsoft Excel, this is usually no problem. Any text typed in a cell that is too small will just spill over into the next cell only if the next cell is empty. However, if the next cell contains data (any kind of information), then the data in the cell before it will look like part of it is cut off, or truncated, at the cell's border. This can be fixed quickly and easily. To widen a column, follow these steps:

1. Move the **mouse pointer** over to the line between the headers of the column you want to widen. When the mouse pointer reaches the line, it changes from a hollow cross into a double headed solid arrow.

2. Press and **hold down the left mouse** button and drag the border line of the column header to the right until all of its entries appears the way you like, or

3. After step one above, simply **double-click** to size each column automatically to fit its largest entry. This is known as **AutoFit.**

Format Headings

It is a good practice to always distinguish headers from the rest of your worksheet. We did a little bit of this earlier in the *Microsoft Word* section. Now let us try it again using the **Format Cells** dialogue window. The steps required to achieve this simple goal are hereby explained:

1. Select or highlight the cell or range of cells you want to format. In our case, move your mouse to **A1**, hold down the **Shift** key on your keyboard and press the **Right Arrow** key on your keyboard until your entire heading from "Patient ID to Clinician" are highlighted.

2. Click **Format** → **Cells** and then choose the **Font** tab

3. Under **Font**, scroll down and pick **Times New Roman.** Under **Font Style**, click **Bold**, go to **Size**, scroll down and pick **11**, and finally, click the box under **Color** and from the drop down color palette, click **White**

4. Click the **Patterns** tab and from the color palette, pick **Dark Blue**

5. Click **Ok.** When you finished, your database headings should look like the following:

Patient ID	First Name	Last Name	SS Number	D O B	Admission Date	Age	Clinician
JL9999	Judy	Lombardi	021-32-9999	7/24/1988	2/22/2003	16	Mindbender, MD
LF9898	Lori	Forget	023-57-9898	3/21/1990	1/22/2003	14	Langhorne, MD
MB9797	Michael	Bordini	781-77-9797	4/30/1981	3/1/2003	23	Middletown, MD

Define or Restrict column(s) in database

In Microsoft Excel, you have the option to define or restrict a column or columns as needed depending on your corporate policy or a specific need. This is a logical thing to do most especially if you are in an environment where many people are entering data into the same data base at the same time or at different times. Follow these steps to define and restrict some of the columns in the database we are creating for MidMed.

1. Move your mouse to column **A2** click and type this formula: **=Left(B2)&Left(C2)&Right(D2,4)**. I'm quite sure you remember this formula from Volume One of Microsoft Office for Healthcare Professionals.

2. Click column **E2**, and then click **Data** → **Validation** and that should lead you to the following **Data Validation** window:

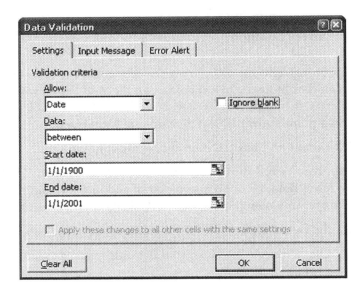

3. Under **Validation criteria**, click the **Allow** box to select **Date**

4. Click on the **Start date** and type this date: **01/01/1900**

5. In the **End date** box, type **01/01/2001**

6. Click the **Input Message** tab.

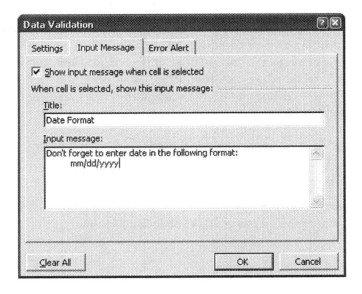

7. Type *"Date Format"* in the **Title** input box, press the **Tab** key to go to the next input box

8. In the **Input message** box, type: *"Don't forget to enter date in the following format: mm/dd/yyyy."* After that,

9. Click the **Error Alert** tab and

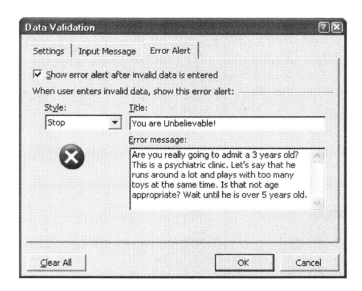

10. In the **Title,** type *"You are Unbelievable."*

11. In the **Error message** box, type these words:

   "Are you really going to admit a 3 year old? This is a psychiatric clinic. Let's say that he runs around a lot and plays with too many toys at the same time. Is that not age appropriate? Wait until he is over 5 years old."

12. Click **Ok** to complete this data validation process.

13. Go back to your database and move your mouse over to **G2** and type this formula: **=DatedIf(E2,Today(),"Y").**

Let us carefully examine what we just did.

• We asked the system to generate **Patient ID** automatically by using what we call concatenation. We asked the system to take the first letter of the first name and add the first letter of the last name plus the last four digit of the social security number.

- In the **D O B** column, we instructed the system not to allow the intake office to admit any child who is not yet 5 years old (this could have been better handled using programming codes).

- Finally, in the **Age** column (the one you are familiar with), it is always good to keep track of the ages of our patients.

Notepad

Wow! It is amazing that we typed that message in step 10 above. Anyway, that kind of message is not recommended in anyway, shape or form. It was designed to amuse you—that's all. When you are actually dealing with the real thing, try to be friendly.

Anyway, we can now move on to the next level and that is to add information to the database.

Add Records

It is easy to add records, or make changes to a database directly in the worksheet. But when you have a large database, keeping track of what row and which column to modify may be difficult at times. Not only that, it is easy to make mistakes such as inadvertently delete predefined formula or restrictions. It is therefore not a good practice to type directly into your database. Always use the data form to add records

A data form gives you a familiar environment of a typical dialog box to work with. With a data form, it is easy to make changes without running into costly mistakes. You can also use it to locate a record quickly and easily. To add a new record to our database, such as a new patient, etc,

1. Click **any cell** in the second row. This is necessary due to the fact that we currently do not have any record in this database, otherwise, it would not have mattered which row and cell you click.

2. Click **Data → Form** and that should bring up the following input **Admission** window:

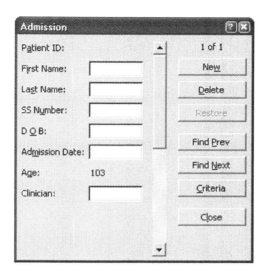

First of all, let me explain how we got the **Admission** form. You remember when we created the **Patient Information** database using the **Template Wizard,** we typed the word *"Admission"* in the **Sheet** dialog box. This was done in the **Template Wizard, step 3 of 5.** When we opened the same database in order to add records, the database is showing one worksheet instead of the usual three worksheets Excel is expected to display by default. The only worksheet currently showing in our **Patient Information** database is named **Admission,** hence the **Admission** forms.

As to why the *Patient ID* and the *Age* fields are not accessible on the Admission form, as you would recollect, we predefined these two field in the section entitled **Define or Restrict Column(s) in database,** we typed specific formulas in both the **Patient ID** and **Age** columns to let the system know in what format we prefer to have the patient id as well as what age limit should be in the *"Age"* column. In that wise, neither of the two columns can be accessed directly from the **Admission** form. Not only that, we also define the field representing date of birth (DOB). As stated earlier, this type of column restriction can be handled better through the use of programming codes but for now we are just going to accept the little we are able to accomplish using point and click.

Now let us enter the following patient information into the **Admission** form:

First Name: Judy

Last Name: Lombardi

SS Number: 021-32-9999

D O B: 07/24/1988

Admission Date: 02/01/2003

Clinician: Mindbender, MD

First Name: Lakita

Last Name: Michael

SS Number: 032-37-9898

D O B: 03/11/2001

Admission Date: 02/24/2003

Clinician: LuckyYou, MD

The system should be able to supply input required in **Patient ID** as well as **Age** cells. However, the information entered for "Wendy" in the **D O B** cell would lead to the activation of the following annoying popup window with attitude:

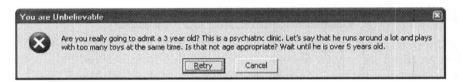

The system will only accept one of the two records. It will only accept Judy Lombardi. Wendy is too young to be admitted into this clinic and this is a matter of policy not necessarily a clinically sound decision. If I were you, I would go back and edit that popup message. Anyway, let's add more records by reproducing the following—always use the **Admission** data form:

Patient ID	First Name	Last Name	SS Number	D O B	Admission Date	Age	Clinician
JL9999	Judy	Lombardi	021-32-9999	7/24/1988	2/1/2003	14	Mindbender, MD
LF9898	Lori	Forget	023-57-9898	3/21/1990	1/22/2003	13	Langhorne, MD
MB9797	Michael	Bordini	781-77-9797	4/30/1981	3/1/2003	21	Middletown, MD
JB9696	Jeniffer	Bristol	521-44-9696	12/24/1991	3/11/2003	11	Mindbender, MD
LW9595	Lisa	Walawala	610-21-9595	3/25/1987	2/10/2003	16	Langhorne, MD
LR9494	Lolita	Ringleader	521-45-9494	10/23/1992	2/27/2003	10	Middletown, MD
MC9393	Moisha	Cityview	032-47-9393	11/24/1988	1/27/2003	14	Mindbender, MD
RN9292	Ryan	Norristown	022-35-9292	9/21/1993	2/26/2003	9	Mindbender, MD
KS9191	Kevin	Salem	341-87-9191	7/30/1991	2/23/2003	11	Middletown, MD
LM9090	Lisa	Morrisville	845-21-9090	5/24/1984	3/21/2003	18	Langhorne, MD
JL8888	Jose	Lehigh	408-43-8888	6/24/1990	3/12/2003	12	Mindbender, MD

Modify Records

In case you need to make changes to an existing record in your database, you can easily do it using the data form. Let's assume that the date of birth for Lisa Morrisville was actually 1994 and not 1984 as previous entered, to modify her record, follow these steps:

1. Click any cell within the database

2. Choose **Data → Form** and scroll down to Lisa's record. You can also use **Find Next** to locate Lisa's record.

3. Click in the **D O B** field to change 1984 to 1994

4. After all the changes are made, click **Close**

Sort Data

Sorting data in a large database is highly unavoidable in some business environment. Sorting a database makes it easier to isolate a group of information. In some cases, it may become necessary to sort patient database to isolate every patient belonging to a particular clinician. Let's assume that Dr. Langhorne would like to know his patient case load. Perhaps this is highly important to him due to the fact that he would like to make time for his family or perhaps reduce his case load for health reasons. Whatever the reason, sorting data in Microsoft Excel is as easy as point and click. To sort data (isolate a group of information) follow these simple steps:

Multilevel Sort

1. Click any cell in the database

2. Click **Data → Sort** and that should bring out the following **Sort** Window

3. Under **Sort by,** click to select the first field (or key) for your sort. In this case, let's select **Patient ID** and don't forget to let the system know if you want to sort in **Ascending** or **Descending** order.

4. Select the second field—**Last Name** and then click **Ascending** or **Descending**

5. Select the third field to sort by—**Clinician** and click **Ascending** or **Descending**

Even though the database arrangement has changed by grouping each Clinician case load one after another, that did not isolate the case load of Dr. Langhorne. Before we address that issue, let us look into a much simpler way we could have performed the sort and that is through a single level sort.

Perform a single level sort

1. Click the field by which you want to sort. In this case, let us click the **Clinician** field

2. Click the **Sort Ascending** button ![sort ascending icon] on the Standard toolbar to sort the clinician column in ascending order, or

3. Click the **Sort Descending** button ![sort descending icon] on the Standard toolbar to sort the column in descending order.

Filter Data in a Database

To truly isolate the patient caseload of Dr. Langhorne, we are going to employ the use of an Excel feature known as **Filter**. When you ask Excel to *Filter* a database, it responds by displaying only the records that match the criteria you select and the rest of the record will be completely out of view temporarily. In that wise, you can choose to print the displayed records or simply send them into a separate worksheet. To isolate all the patient of Dr. Langhorne using the process of filtering, follow these steps:

1. Click any cell in the database
2. Choose **Data → Filter → AutoFilter**

As you can see, Excel adds an arrow to the right of each field in your database. To complete your database filtering, all you need to do is click the arrow next to the *Clinician* field to activate its drop down list. A list should appear showing the following information:

> [All]
> [Top 10...]
> [Custom]
> Langhorne, MD
> Middletown, MD
> Mindbender, MD

Try and click on **Langhorne, MD** and that should isolate and display the current patient caseload of Dr. Langhorne with the remaining part of the database temporarily out of view. If you are wondering as to the purpose of the first three fields, they are as following:

[All]   Displays all the records for that field, it will take you back to where you were before the filtering option.

[Top 10...]   Displays the top 10 of the clinician record you select from the dialog

[Custom]   Displays records according to the criteria you specify. You might want to use this option to display only patients that are equal to or greater than 10 years old.

Delete Records

You can quickly delete from your database, any record you no longer need. When this is done using the data form, any range such as sum previously defined by the database will be automatically adjusted. To delete a record

1. Click any cell within the database

2. Go to **Data → Form**

3. Scroll to the record you want to delete and click **Delete**

4. Choose **Ok** to confirm the deletion. Do the same (repeat the above steps) to delete additional records as needed.

5. Click **Close**

Add or Delete Worksheets

Each workbook usually gives you three worksheets by default. Depending on your need, you can add more worksheets or delete extra sheets if you like. However, using the Template Wizard to create our database would have forced the system to give you one worksheet, only, to work with.

To add more, follow these steps:

1. Click the existing worksheet tab

2. Choose **Insert → Worksheet**

To delete a worksheet

1. Click the tab of the worksheet you would like to remove

2. Choose **Edit → Delete Sheet**

3. Click **Ok**

Rename a Worksheet

In case the name you gave a worksheet is not descriptive enough, you have the option to rename. One thing you have to understand is that using a descriptive name will help you and other users to quickly identify the type of data contained on each sheet. Follow these steps to rename a worksheet:

1. Double-click the tab of the worksheet you want to rename

2. Type the new name for the worksheet and you will discover that what you type replaces the existing name

3. Press the **Enter** key

Notepad

Another way to **Add, Delete,** or **Rename** a worksheet is to right-click on the sheet tab. A shortcut menu appears. From the shortcut menu, you can select **Insert** to add new worksheet, or **Delete** to remove any unwanted worksheet, or **Rename** to change the name of the worksheet to something more descriptive.

The truth about the Template Wizard

Needless to say, the template wizard is good and very helpful but could you believe that you seriously do not need it to create a database template! Microsoft intentionally left it out of *Excel 2002* for a reason and placed it on a remote Internet Island. Unless you are led to where it is by one of the citizens of this island (like I did a little while ago), you will never know where it is. But no matter what the reason for Microsoft not including it in *Excel 2002*, it is always good to know how to use it. Let's face it, how would you feel if you are in one of these IT conferences or meetings with your girlfriend or your wife, and this strange looking guy walks up to you, telling you about how he created the best database in the universe with the help of the **Template Wizard**! And the most beautiful woman standing next to you is going really! And you are scratching your head trying to figure out what in the universe is this stranger up to! Now you can let whoever it is know that *Direct Approach* (DA) is better.

What is Direct Approach?

As defined earlier, a database is a collection of records. Each record contains related information about a single item such as an employee. Each record is divided into fields such as the employee's first name, last name, social security number, phone number, address, city, state, zip code, etc. With *Excel 2002*, you can create any database by entering the fields name directly onto your Excel worksheet. This is what **Direct Approach** is all about. It is the fastest way to create a database outside of the **Template Wizard.** To try out **DA,** follow these steps:

1. Open Microsoft Excel

2. Click **A1** and type your database field names directly (as specified earlier) onto **worksheet1** beginning at column **A1** and use the tab key to move from column **A1** to **B1** and so on and so forth.

3. Adjust and format each column as necessary

   a. Select the field names and click **Format → Cell**

   b. Click the **Font** tab and under **Font Style**, select **Bold**, under **Size**, select **11** and under color, select **White**.

   c. Click **Patterns** tab and select **Dark Green**

   d. Click **Ok**

4. Enter necessary formulas to define the appropriate fields such as **Patient ID** and **Age**.

5. Move the insertion block to the column under the **D O B** field and click **Data → Validation** and follow the previous steps outlined earlier for **Data Validation**

6. Click **Data → Form** to populate your database.

About the guy at the IT conference, now you can say to him: hey pal! you could have avoided using such a long and time consuming process, and just type your database field directly into your worksheet, save it as a template and when the time comes, use the data **Form** to populate your database. Guess who would be going, really! One more thing, tell him to go and get a copy of this book *"Microsoft Office for Healthcare Professionals."*

> "You cannot achieve a new goal by applying the same level of thinking that got you where you are today."
>
> Albert Einstein

Chapter Sixteen

Formulas and Functions

Objectives

When you finish this chapter, you will be able to:

- Differentiate between formulas and functions
- Create and perform complex formulas
- Evaluate formulas one expression at a time
- Describe different kinds of cell references in formulas
- Use IF and the LOOKUP functions
- Use the watch window
- Generate random numbers
- Perform statistical analysis

One of the most amazing features of Excel is its ability to help people solve number problems. With formulas, you can perform any calculation based on a data set. The type of calculations you can perform ranges from just a simple calculation such as adding a block of numbers to dealing with complex calculation such as trying to determine monthly payment on a $125,000 mortgage loan amortized over a period of 30 years at 5.75% interest rate.

In chapter one, you learned how to perform those simple calculations and here we are going to take it a step further by showing you how to create and perform complex formulas.

On the other hand, a function is a preprogrammed calculation. All you need to do is recall the function and provide it with some information using the proper syntax and when this is done, it is certain the system would give you the expected answer. For example, let us try to calculate monthly payment on the mortgage scenario created in paragraph one above.

Description	Data
Annual Interest Rate	5.75%
Number of months of payments	360
Amount of Loan	$125,000.00
Monthly Payment	$729.47

In this scenario, I am going to use a function known as **PMT** for payment function, and instruct the system to perform calculations using the correct order of operations =**PMT(B2/12,B3,B4**. Now, let us look carefully at the formula in the light of the only function employed.

1. I recalled the PMT function (don't forget, every formula must begin with the equal (=) sign.

2. I then instructed the system to take the annual interest rate and divide it by the number of months per year.

3. The next step is to simply follow the format required by Excel 2002. The total number of payments is actually taken from the number of months per year multiplied by the number of years representing the duration of the loan which is 12*30 = 360.

4. The last item on the formula based on the function is to supply the loan amount which is $125,000.

5. If the monthly payment shows a negative number instead of positive, simply add negative sign (minus sign) after the equal (=) sign but before the **PMT** function and the result would come out as positive number. When you finish typing the formula, it should look like the following: = -PMT(B2/12,B3,B4)

How to Calculate Amortization

	A	B	C	D	E
1	Number of Years	30			
2	Interest Rate	5.87%			
3	Principal	125000			
4	Payment	=-PMT(b2/12,b1*12,b3)			
5					
6	Balance	Interest	Principal Paid	Pre-Paid	New Balance
7	=b3	=a7*b2/12	=b4-b7	100	=a7-c7-d7
8	=e7	=a8*b2/12	=b4-b8	100	=a8-c8-d8
9	=e8	=a9*b2/12	=b4-b9	100	=a9-c9-d9

6. Copy down the last row one column at a time beginning at A9 followed by B9, C9, D9 and E9.

How to evaluate formulas one expression at a time

A formula may appear to be entered correctly but the order of the functions or operations may not be correct. To be sure you will always get the expected result, Microsoft includes a friendly feature that will allow you to evaluate formulas and this feature is known as (guess what!) **Evaluate Formula.** When it comes to assessing every part of a formula, most especially nested formulas, there is no better tool. Evaluate Formula is designed to help you zero in on the specific part of a formula that may not be working the way you expect.

Every programmer is familiar with debugging tool available in programming environment. Evaluate Formula works the same in Excel environment. Let's say we have a database that looks like the following:

First Quarter Cash Flow Need		
Period	**Cash on hand**	**Account Receivable**
January	8848	35478
February	7984	27934
March	2932	42581
Evaluation	105993	

We enter the following formula in cell B7:

$$=IF(AVERAGE(B3:B5)<55000,SUM(C3:C5),0)$$

The result revealed the total of our Account Receivable because Cash on hand is less than $55,000. Let us look carefully at the structure of our formula and you will discover that what we are trying to do is determine if we are going to see the bank manager for a line of credit or go for receivable factoring in the light of our strong Account Receivable (AR). The formula says: if the average of the values in cells B3 through B5 is less than $55,000 then evaluate and give us the sum of the values in cells C3 through C5, otherwise, return 0. In other words, we would like to know if the average of our cash on hand for the first quarter is less than $55,000. If that is the case, the second part of our formula is asking the system to tell us the current face value of our account receivable. To use the *Evaluate Formula* feature in Excel, follow these steps:

1. Click **Tools → Formula Auditing → Evaluate Formula** and that should lead you to the following dialog window

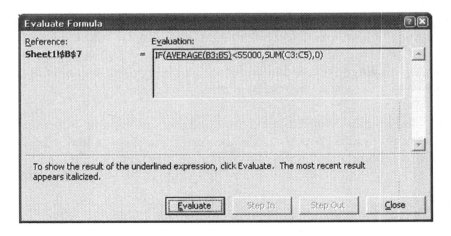

2. To show the result of the underlined expression, click **Evaluate** and that should produce the result of the first part of the formula as follows:

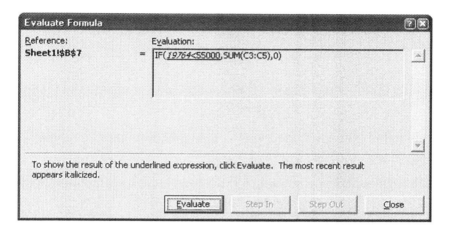

3. The first part of the expression reveals an average value of $19,764 which is less than $55,000.

4. Click **Evaluate** again to see the result of the second part. This second part simply evaluates to true or false in the light of the overall value of our account receivable which in this case is $105,993.

Notepad

If you are using Excel 2002 otherwise known as Excel XP, there is another option called **Show Calculation Steps.** This is available on the **Error Checking Options** smart tag menu. Basically, this option operates in a way similar to Evaluate Formula. However the only difference is that the first expression is already evaluated when the dialog box is displayed.

Let us take it one step further by changing the value of our Cash Flow for each month, thereby producing an average greater than $55,000. What do you think would be the result in response to our formula? What this means is that there is no need, right now, to borrow or rush out in favor of receivable factoring. The panic level is equal to **Zero** because the average of our cash flow for the three periods revealed is greater than **$55,000** and the same with AR. In this case, we are doing fine.

	First Quarter Cash Flow Need	
Period	Cash on hand	Account Receivable
January	51879	35478
February	56545	27934
March	62954	42581
Evaluation	0	

Name Box

At the top of Excel gridline, to the right of the formula bar is where you will find the name box. Name box displays the address of the active cell. If your insertion block is in **A1**, the name box will read A1. To put simply, the main purpose of the name box is to display the address of the active cell but you can use the Name box to name a cell or group of cells. Instead of A1, B2, C34, D23, and so on and so forth, you can give each cell a more descriptive name. When a cell is given a name, you can refer to it from anywhere within your worksheet without having to worry about its cell number. It provides a more efficient way to handle cell referencing within formulas and functions. For example, let us take a careful look at the following calculations:

Income	Monthly Total
Full Time	$3,875.00
Part Time	962.00
Consulting Services	1,174.00
Total Income	6,011.00

1. Click cell **B2** and the Name box should read B2

2. To replace the B2 with a more descriptive name, click on the **Name** box and the B2 showing should be highlighted right away

3. Type **Full_Time** to replace the B2 name

4. Click cell **B3** and in the Name box type **Part_Time**

5. Click cell **B4** and also in the Name box, type **Consulting** and finally

6. Click cell **B5** and type **Total_Income** in the Name box.

Please note that in typing those names, I typed underscore instead of space. The use of space would have resulted in syntax error. This shall be explained in full when we get to programming in Visual Basic for Applications (VBA).

Notepad

Even though I did not specifically ask you to type the labels in column A, it is highly recommended that you include both the headings and all the information in column A. The information you input into column "A" is strictly *Labels* and the one typed into the Name box for column B represents *Cell Reference*.

Now that we have changed the cell name reference, let us enter the formula for Total Income as follows: **=Full_Time+Part_Time+Consulting**

Cell References in Formulas

Here, I am going to discuss three different kinds of cell references. They are: Relative, Absolute, and Mixed cell references. Anything about statistics and the discussion of the steps leading to the conclusion of statistical analysis are relatively boring to most people but highly essential in life and when the time comes, most people usually wish they had paid attention to all its nitty-gritty.

Absolute Reference

Most of the formulas I have used up to this point had been **Relative Reference** formulas. For example, suppose you have a worksheet like the following:

	A	B	C
1		January	February
2	Brooklyn Clinic	67954	72836
3	Princeton Clinic	58721	63147
4	Philadelphia Clinic	64121	68932
5	Total	=Sum(B2:B4)	

When you copy the formula in cell B5 to cell C5, you will discover that the references has changed to =Sum(C2:C4) and the same thing would happen when you copy further to cell D5. It will immediately assume appropriate cell references and the formula would look like this =Sum(D2:D4). This is due to the fact that a relative cell points *only* to a cell position *relative* to the formula's location. To put simply, each time you copy a formula with relative cell references, the formula along with its references will adjust automatically to reflect its new position.

Absolute Reference

There are times when you would not want the references to be adjusted automatically to avoid getting an incorrect answer or in some cases, an error message. For example, let us take another look at the same worksheet:

	A	B	C	D
1		January	February	Percentage of January Sales
2	Brooklyn Clinic	67954	72836	=B2/$B$5
3	Princeton Clinic	58721	63147	
4	Philadelphia Clinic	64121	68932	
5	Total	=Sum(B2:B4)		

Please bear in mind that an **Absolute cell reference** clearly defines the cell you would not want adjusted when you copy the formula. To create absolute cell reference, the rule of thumb is to type a **$** (dollar sign) in front of both the column letter and row number of the cell you want to see remain constant. The formula in the worksheet above reads: **=B2/$B$5** as oppose to **=B2/B5**. There is no doubt that **=B2/B5** would have given us the correct answer in column **D2** only. But when the same formula is copied to cell **D3**, it will adjust automatically to: **=B3/B6**, thereby result in an incorrect answer or error message if column **B6** is an empty column. To avoid this kind of incorrect answer or error message, we employed the use of absolute cell reference.

An absolute cell reference simply does not adjust when the original formula is copied to a new column. In this case, the formula **=B2/$B$5** would produce correct answer in **D2** and when the same formula is copied to cell **D3**, the new formula would read; **=B3/$B$5** and also produce a correct answer. The only absolute part of this formula is the divisor and the divisor in our example is the *Total* sale for the month of January.

Mixed Cell References

On the other hand, there are instances whereby you would not want to keep an entire column absolute. In that case, all you need to do is employ the use of **mixed cell references.** A mixed cell reference is a reference in which only part of the cell—perhaps the column letter or row number is absolute as in $B5 or B$5. For example, let us recall the same worksheet to calculate the percentage of February sales. We are going to change the formula in **D2** to **=B2/B$5** as in the following:

	A	B	C	D	E
1		January	February	Percentage of January Sales	Percentage of February Sales
2	Brooklyn Clinic	67954	72836	=B2/B$5	
3	Princeton Clinic	58721	63147		
4	Philadelphia Clinic	64121	68932		
5	Total	=Sum(B2:B4)	=Sum(C2:C4)		

As you are well aware by now, when the formula in cell **D2** is copied to cell **D3**, it changes to **=B3/B$5**. Let us look carefully at the anatomy of our formula. In the first cell reference, the row number is relative, in that wise, it is adjusted by one due to the fact that the formula was copied one row down. However, the second cell reference (**B$5**), is not adjusted because it is absolute. But when the same formula is copied across to cell **E2**, the formula will change to =C2/C$5. One interesting thing here is how the column letter has changed in both cell references because it is relative.

Number Formats

Each time you enter a number into an unformatted cell, Excel displays the number exactly as entered. If you enter 52978.00 Excel will display the number and drop the trailing zeros after the decimal point. Not only that, if your number is larger than the cell, it is highly likely Excel will change it into scientific notation format. If you are an Accountant, you would want your negative number to reflect the actual result of your computation. For example, some individuals are especially concerned about how negative numbers are displayed—some would prefer to see negative numbers display in red while others would prefer to use parenthesis or perhaps simply show a minus sign before the numbers. Regardless of your preferences, Excel makes it easier for you to format numbers in a variety of ways. Number formats can only change the way numbers are displayed but not the actual numbers. To format numbers, do the following:

1. Highlight all the cells containing the numbers you want to format.

2. Click **Format** → **Cells...**and that should take you to the following window:

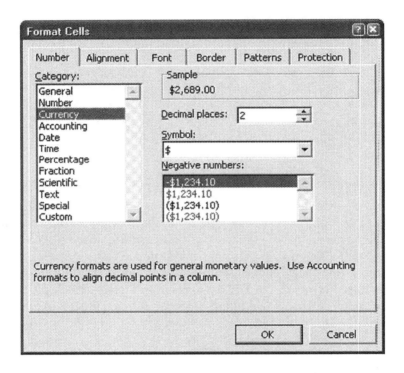

3. Click the **Number** tab (if not already activated) and you will see all the choices under **Category**. There you will find choices that allow you to apply the currency, comma, or percentage number style.

IF Function and the Lookup Functions

Depending on the structure of your worksheets, there are some functions designed to help you make decisions based upon the values entered in another cell. One of those functions is the **IF** function. The result returned by the **IF** function is dependent upon whether a logical condition is true or false. Other functions include **HLOOKUP** and **VLOOKUP**. Both of these functions return values from lookup tables.

IF Function

If you are a payroll specialist who is concerned about payroll deductions, making sure that they are calculated properly and appropriately, and that each employee's paycheck reflects their true compensation, you will find these functions helpful. If you are an accounting manager endowed with the task of making sure the correct commission is paid at the right time to your medical and surgical supplies/equipments sales force, you will find these functions helpful. The **IF** function uses a logical operator such as > (**greater than**) or < (**less than**) to evaluate a condition. Any of the following logical operators can be used with the **IF** function:

Logical Operator	Description
=	Equal
<	Less Than
>	Greater Than
>=	Greater than or equal to
<=	Less than or equal to
<>	Not equal to

The general syntax of the **IF** function is =**IF(Comparison, True, False)**. In a real world, it would be difficult to find employee who will work for commission if the rule is too strict and highly inflexible. For example, if you are trying to motivate your sales team to sell $10,000 and make 15% commission (very generous pay by the way) but offers no commission when individual sale is less than $10,000, you may find yourself doing all the work alone and your time is fractured between having to do administrative work as well as attending to customers. On the other hand, if you create an environment whereby members of your sales team are compensated using graduated commission table, you would not only sell a lot, somehow, you would discover that you have one of the best sales team in the industry. The following is an example of a graduated commission table paying 15% commission if sales is >= 10,000. To produce expected result, enter the following into your Excel worksheet:

	A	B	C	D	E
1	Monthly Commission Calculations				
2	February 2003 Report				
3					
4	Medical Equipment	February	Com. Rate	Total Com.	Evaluation
5	Bob Doe	12000			
6	Rick Maldonado	8957			
7	Tanisha Brown	14721			
8	Michael Douglas	9897			

1. Enter the information presented in column **A1**, **A2**, and skip **A3**

2. Complete the headings in Row 4. Enter Medical Equipment in **A4**, February in **B4**, Com. Rate in **C4**, Total Com in **D4** and Evaluation in **E4**

3. Enter employee's names in column **A** beginning at A5

4. Enter sales figures in column **B** directly across from each name

5. In column **C5**, enter this formula **=IF(B5>=10000,15%,10%)** and use the fill handle to copy the formula to **C6**, **C7** and **C8**

6. Enter this formula **=B5*C5** in column **D5** and use the fill handle to copy the formula to **D6**, **D7** and **D8**. When you finish, your Excel worksheet should look like the following:

Monthly Commission Calculations				
February 2003 Report				
Medical Equipment	February	Commission Rate	Total Commission	Evaluation
Bob Doe	12,000.00	15%	1,800.00	
Rick Maldonado	8,957.00	10%	895.70	
Tanisha Brown	14,721.00	15%	2,208.15	
Michael Douglas	9,897.00	10%	989.70	

Evaluate the IF Function to return text result

We have used the IF function to return percentage result. We are now going to use the IF function to return text result. It is easier for some people to understand statistical results produced in plain English more than the statistical result produced in percentage. In the next exercise, under "Evaluation," the IF function will return the phrase "Below Quota" when sales are less than $10,000 and "Above Quota" when sales are greater than or equal to $10,000. Let us enter the following IF function in cell **E5**: **=IF(B5>=10000,"Above Quota","Below Quota")**. Do not forget to include the quotation mark. Once the formula for the new IF function is entered in E5, use the fill handle to copy the formula down to cells E6, E7 and E8. Also, do not forget to highlight Cells E5 down to E8 and click **Align Right** on the Formatting toolbar. Your final statistical result should look like the following:

Monthly Commission Calculations				
February 2003 Report				
Medical Equipment	February	Commission Rate	Total Commission	Evaluation
Bob Doe	12,000.00	15%	1,800.00	Above Quota
Rick Maldonado	8,957.00	10%	895.70	Below Quota
Tanisha Brown	14,721.00	15%	2,208.15	Above Quota
Michael Douglas	9,897.00	10%	989.70	Below Quota

Vlookup Function

The **VLOOKUP** otherwise known as the Vertical Lookup and the **HLOOKUP** also known as the Horizontal Lookup functions are designed to look up values in tables such as tax tables, commission rate tables and any other tables. The syntax for the **VLOOKUP** which is used more often is =**VLOOKUP(search argument, lookup table, column number)**. Let us take a careful look at the VLOOKUP function and its components in the following worksheet:

	A	B	C	D
1	Sales	February Sales	Commission Rate	Evaluation
2	Ryan Michael	12,500		
3				
4				

5	Sales Volume	Commission Rate	Evaluation
6	-	0%	Under Achiever
7	8,000	10%	Below Quota
8	10,000	15%	Below Quota
9	15,000	15%	Above Quota
10	20,000	22%	Above Quota
11	25,000	25%	Over Achiever

There are two major parts to this worksheet—the outcome part which you will find between **A1** and **D2** and the lookup table located between **A5** and **C11**. The lookup table is more like a storage area and can be located anywhere (possibly out of sight) within the same worksheet as the outcome portion. By the same token, you can also keep the lookup table on a separate worksheet.

The use of Watch Window

The **Watch Window** provides a way for you to see what is going on in another cell without having to scroll to the actual cell. For example, let's say you are entering data in cell **A89** which is likely to affect the result of a formula you entered in cell C12. Instead of scrolling back to cell C12 to see the result of the formula, you can actually see the value of the formula change from within the watch window even if you are currently entering data in cell A89.

Not only that, with the help of the *Watch Window*, you can even watch values on other sheets or in other workbooks. To activate the **Watch Window**, follow these steps:

1. Right-click the cell where you are currently entering data
2. Click **Add Watch** and that would immediately activate the **Watch Window**
3. On the **Watch Window**, click **Add Watch** and that should lead you to the following popup dialog box:

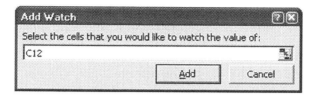

4. Type the cell address where you entered the formula and

5. Click **Add** and that should lead to a result similar to the following

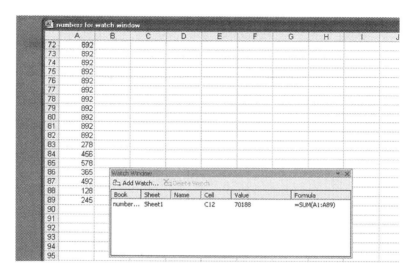

Generate Random Numbers.

When the contents of an Excel spreadsheet are not given, you can use randomly generated numbers to quickly populate the spreadsheet. There is a function specially designed to make generating numbers randomly easy to accomplish. This function is known as RAND function. To use it, follow these steps:

1. Click any cell to produce a number between 0 and 1 and type =**RAND**(), or

2. Click any cell (usually cell **A1** if this is a blank worksheet) to generate a number between 1 and 100, type =**RAND**()*100.

3. To populate a spreadsheet, use the fill handle as following to quickly populate as many cells as you'd like with random numbers:

   a. Click the cell where the first number appears.

   b. Move your mouse to the bottom right corner of the insertion block—right on top of the little dark square block and your cursor will then turn into a little plus sign.

   c. While your mouse is on the tinny dark square block, click and hold down the left mouse button and drag across to cover as many cells as you want

   d. Repeat steps **3b** and **3c** above but drag down the mouse to cover as many cells and release the mouse when you are done.

Notepad

To change the number format of your random numbers (for example, if you'd prefer whole numbers to decimal points), click **Cells** on the **Format** menu. In the Format Cells dialog box, click the **Number** tab and then click **Number** in the **Category** list. Then in the **Decimal places** box, enter the number zero and click **Ok.**

Tools to perform a statistical analysis

I just want to bring to your attention the fact that you can use Microsoft Excel to assist you in your quest for accurate statistical analysis. My intent is not to teach statistical analysis but to let you know that these tools are available should you need to use them. Most of what you will need is available in one of Excel features known as **Data Analysis**. It is highly likely that *Data Analysis* may not be available to use right away. This does not mean you bought the wrong version of Microsoft Excel. It simply means that you will have to add *Data Analysis* to your system. To install and use *Data Analysis* Add in, follow these steps:

1) On the **Tools** menu, click **Data Analysis**. If **Data Analysis** is not available, you will need to load the *Analysis ToolPak*. To do that, follow the steps below:

   (i) On the **Tools** menu, click **Add-Ins.**

   (ii) In the **Add-Ins available** list, select the **Analysis ToolPak** box, and then click **OK**. Go back to step One.

2) When you see the following **Data Analysis** dialog box pops up,

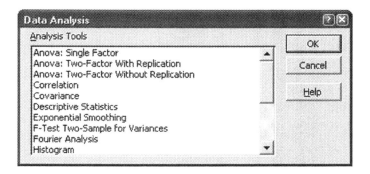

3) Click the name of the analysis tool you want to use, and then click **OK**.

4) Each analysis tool would lead you to a dialog box for the tool you selected in order to set the analysis options you want.

The following example is taken from an actual record of some outpatient medical clinics and the data are recorded in million. It is hereby presented with the intent to explain how best to handle calculating standard deviation in Excel spreadsheet. Lower standard deviation is usually regarded as an indicator of stability while higher standard deviation is regarded as higher volatility.

	A	B	C
1	Year	Average Yearly Visit	Squared Deviation
2	1994	4.9	0.96
3	1995	5.4	0.23
4	1996	5.9	0.00
5	1997	5.1	0.60
6	1998	5.6	0.08
7	1999	5.8	0.01
8	2000	6.9	1.04
9	2001	6.4	0.27
10	2002	6.9	1.04
11		Total of Column "C"	4.24

The formula for the Squared Deviation typed in cell C2 is: =**(B2-AVERAGE(B$2:B$10))^2** and to get the Standard Deviation, type either of the following formulas in cell C11:

=STDEVA(B$2:B$10) or =SQRT(C11/(COUNT(B2:B10)-1))

A step by step calculation is as follows:

1. You first of all calculate Average of the data set **=AVERAGE(B$2:B$10)**

2. Subtract the average from each year data to find deviation **=B2-AVERAGE(B$2:B$10)**

3. You use the exponential operator which in this case is the ^ (**caret**) sign to obtain the square root of step 2 above **=(B2-AVERAGE(B$2:B$10))^2**

4. Try and obtain the total of the squared deviation using this formula **=SUM(B2:B10)**

5. The formula to obtain the total count of the data set is **=COUNT(B2:B9)-1** and this represents **N-1**

6. We need to divide the squared deviation by the formula in step 5 above. To get that, we have to use this formula **=C11/(COUNT(B2:B10)-1)**

7. Finally, you get the standard deviation using the following formula: **=SQRT(C11/(COUNT(B2:B10)-1))**

8. However, if you are using Excel 2000 or Excel XP (2002), the following is all you need: **=STDEVA(B$2:B$10)**

Notepad

Needless to say, this is just one aspect of statistical analysis and the explanations presented here are somehow insufficient for something this complex unless you are well informed in statistical analysis. Should you like to know more about the subject of Statistical Analysis, feel free to visit www.mednetservices.com from time to time for lots of Free downloads.

> "You become a champion by fighting one more round. When things are tough, you fight one more round."
>
> James Corbett

Chapter Seventeen

Graphics and Charts

Objectives

When you finish this chapter, you will be able to:

- Insert clip arts and pictures in worksheet
- Use the Chart Wizard to create a chart
- Create and work with styles

The focus of a Database is to produce expected result. However, there are times when you might want to dress up the worksheet on which all the nitty-gritty of the database resides. Even though looking good is the last thing on the mind of your database development team, however, a well designed database with appropriate graphic or picture can lead to a whole new attitude, perhaps makes it easier to figure out what the database is all about, thereby eliminate barriers to communication.

> A policeman stops a lady and asks for her license.
> He says "Lady, it says here that you should be wearing glasses."
> The woman answered "Well, I have contacts."
> The policeman replied "I don't care who you know! You're getting a ticket!"
>
> Author unknown

For clarity, *Microsoft Excel* makes it possible to insert clip arts, pictures and even company logo in your worksheet. The program comes with so many useful clip arts and if you cannot find appropriate clip art for your project, you have the option to search online (from within the program) for more clip arts. You can also use your own custom designed graphic; company logo, scanned picture or drawings or any work of art generated digitally or otherwise.

If you have used the clip art gallery in *Microsoft Word*, you are probably familiar with how you can insert from the gallery. Even if you are not too familiar, the process is easy to follow.

Insert Clip Arts and Pictures

1. Increase the width of the column (cell) where you want to insert the clip art or increase the width of every column (if you have to) by doing the following:

    a. To increase the width of every column, click the **Select All** button, the block at the top left corner of the gridline—the empty block between the row number 1 and column letter A.

    b. To increase the width of only one column, click the column, and then

    c. Click **Format → Column → Width** to set the width (in this case, let us set it to 18)

2. Change the font to *Times New Roman* and the font size to 11 (this is optional)

3. Click any of the cells to deselect the entire worksheet.

4. Click the **Insert Clip Art** button on the **Drawing** toolbar usually located at the bottom of your screen (if activated)

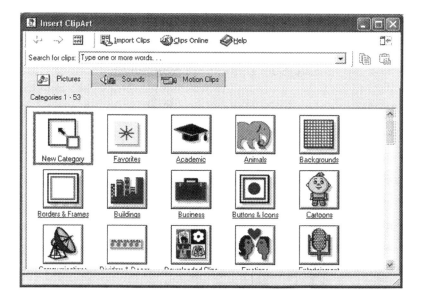 or simply

5. Click **Insert → Picture → Clip Art**—either way would lead you to the following screen:

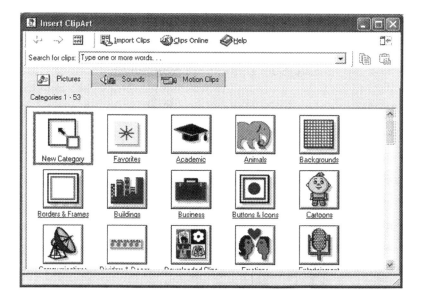

6. Click the **Buildings** category to display clip arts related to buildings most especially if your database is designed to produce amortization or related information

7. Click **any picture** of your choice.

8. Move your mouse over the pop-up menu to see the ScreenTip of each button on the pop-up menu.

9. Click the **Preview clip** option on the popup menu to display an enlarged copy of the clip.

10. Click the **Close** button on the **Preview** window. If this is what you are looking for,

11. Click **Insert** on the pop-up menu to insert the picture in your worksheet.

If the clip art you are looking for is not available among those provided with Microsoft Office, you can always go online to find the appropriate one.

12. Click the **Clips Online** button (before you do that, make sure your computer system is already logged on to the Internet). And that should bring out a dialogue window designed to remind you. Do not forget that connecting to the Internet is necessary and required.

13. Click **Ok** if you are connected.

14. To add your custom designed clip arts, company logo, drawing, etc, click the **Import Clips** to search your system for your company logo, drawing or your unique one-of-a-kind graphic file. Try to reproduce the following example:

RFS, Enterprises
Race For Strength

	Income	Expenses	Net Income
Medicare	$21,875	$12,998	$8,877
Medicaid	$19,894	$11,947	$7,947
HMO	$23,689	$12,947	$10,742
Staffing	$32,169	$11,547	$20,622
	$97,627	$49,439	$48,188

Using the Chart Wizard

There are times when you need to establish comparisons, trends and other relationships. In a way, there are times when you need to help the numbers in a worksheet tell their own story in living color. One of the best ways to convey this is through effective use of charts. A chart can help anyone including those who despise numbers understand the true meaning and relationship between the worksheet data and performance/productivity.

One of the main purposes of a chart is to represent data graphically. Excel makes it possible to create column charts, bar charts, line charts, area charts and pie charts using the Chart Wizard. It also provides a way to edit and format every chart object.

We are going to create a chart with the help of the Chart Wizard from the following worksheet:

	January Sales
Medicare	257895.00
Medicaid	124956.00
HMO	232741.00
Blue Cross	89654.00
C. Ins.	131542.00
Private Pay	46738.00

Create a chart

1. Select the data you want to present graphically as well as the column heading and row label (it is always a good practice to select your data as oppose to defining it during the running of the wizard).

2. Choose **Insert → Chart** or simply click the **Chart Wizard** button on the Toolbar. Either way, you would be led to the following screen from Excel 2000:

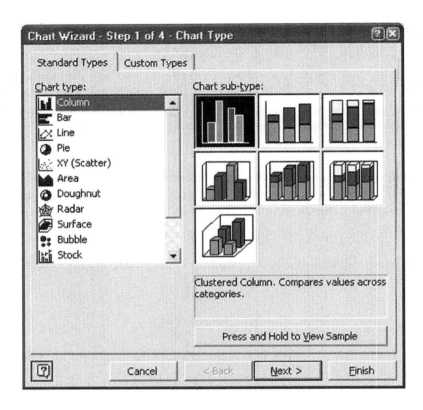

3. Select a chart type from those listed under **Chart Type** and also select a chart sub-type from those listed under **Chart sub-type** (for our sample database, let us pick **Pie** chart).

4. Click **Next** to go to step 2 of 4 of the Chart Wizard. From the step 2 of the Chart Wizard, you will be given the options to choose:

   a. A different range of cells (this is where you define the range if you had not selected your range prior to going into the Chart Wizard).

   b. How to present the chart—Rows or Columns.

5. Click **Next** to go to step 3 of 4. Here you will have the option to enter the **Title,** hide the labels on the category axes when you click the **Axes** tab. Click **Gridlines** tab to decide whether your chart should show gridline for the value axes displayed. Click the **Legend** tab to identify the columns. The **Data Labels** tab displays the values from the worksheet on

top of the columns. And on the **Data Table,** click the **Show data table** check box and a table will appear below the Preview chart.

6. Click **Next** to go to step 4 (the last step) of the **Chart Wizard** and when the step 4 dialogue window appears, you will be giving two choices.

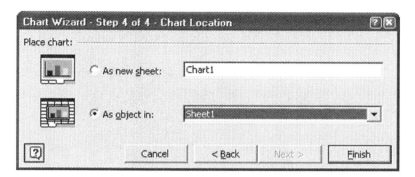

7. Click **As new sheet** to create the chart on a separate sheet, or

8. Click **As object in** to embed the chart in the current worksheet

9. Click **Finish** and your worksheet should look similar to the following:

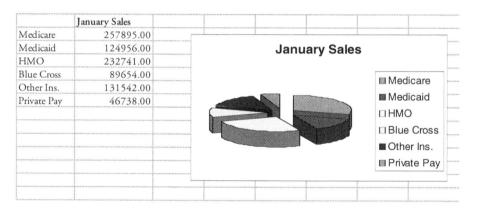

Working with Styles

When we talk about *style* in Excel, we are simply talking about cell formatting. A predefined cell formatting can be applied to any cell. Using styles provides some great advantages in comparison to manual formatting.

1. It provides consistency. Once applied, you no longer need to remember the format settings used for specific types of cells.

2. Styles are more convenient. Using styles makes it possible to create reusable format, thereby avoid the monotony of having to repeat the same formatting commands over and again in various cells.

Microsoft Excel makes it possible to create styles from the following two methods:

1. One method is to create style by example. In this case, you manually pick all of the formatting commands for a particular cell and then assign style name to the formatting.

2. The second method is to create style by definition. This method allows you to open the dialog box, and choose the format settings you would like to assign to the style.

To create Styles by Example:

1. Open the *Admission* database created in chapter two

RFTC Enterprises Mortgage Inc.					
Period	Income				
1st Quarter	23549				
2nd Quarter	26321				
3rd Quarter	27892				
4th Quarter	31875				

2. To add the *Style* button to the Formatting toolbar, right-click on any toolbar and choose **Customize** and then do the following:

    a. Click the **Commands** tab to activate it.

    b. Click **Format** under *Categories*

    c. Drag the **Style** box on to the *Formatting* toolbar and release the mouse.

3. Close the *Customize* dialog box. That is all you need to define a Style by Example. For more information visit: www.mednetservices.com

"We must use time creatively and forever realize that the time is always right to do great things."

Martin L. King, Jr.

Chapter Eighteen

Working with Macros and Toolbars

Objectives

When you finish this chapter, you will be able to:

- Record and run a macro
- Assign a macro to a button

Some of you who bought volume one of *Microsoft Office for Healthcare Professionals* would remember my extensive coverage of Recording and Playing Macros. This is one of many features that are common to all of *Microsoft Office* programs. Needless to say, there are some tasks that are just too long and at times too technical to repeat over and again. In a busy environment, such a lengthy and highly involved task may often-times result in human error unless something is done to reduce the possibility of unnecessary mistakes.

Macro provides a means to create mini-automation without getting into all the nitty-gritty of programming. A macro provides a way to record a set of steps along with its instructions that can be played back at a later time. Excel's macro is capable of recording keystrokes and any associated command necessary to per-form a task.

As you know, creating a database involves a lot of steps. Adding more information to the database shouldn't require so many steps.

1. Open the **Admission** database developed in Chapter Two

2. Choose **Tools** → **Macro** → **Record New Macro**. In the **Macro Name** text box, type a descriptive name in the Macro Name box. Space is an invalid character. Try not to use space in macro names. Let us name the macro *AdmissionMacro*.

3. To assign this macro to a shortcut key, in the Shortcut Key box, type **Q** (this could be any letter of interest to you). The **Ctrl +** would change to **Ctrl + Shift + |**. This is slightly different from the way Microsoft Word handles assigning shortcut keys to macros in Word.

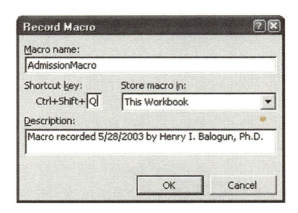

4. In the **Store macro in** box, click to select the location where you want to store the macro. This macro is applicable to the current workbook only. So, we are going to select **This Workbook** option.

5. Click **Ok** to begin recording.

6. Choose **Data → Form**

7. When the data **Form** appears, click **Ok**

8. To stop recording, look for the following hanging toolbar:

9. Click on the **Stop Recording** button (the square blue block) on the toolbar. The macro is now ready to be played back.

Running Macro

Once you have recorded a macro, running it is easy. When we were recording the *AdmissionMacro* macro, we assigned the macro to a shortcut **Ctrl + Shift + Q**. Not only that, we also indicated in the **Store macro in** box that the macro was for **This Workbook**. To run it, make sure that the *Admission* database is open and active on your screen, otherwise it would not work.

Hold down the **Ctrl + Shift** key and press **Q**. The data **Form** screen should pop up.

To run a macro from the **Tools** menu, follow these steps:

1. Open the document in which you want to run the macro—in this case, open the *Admission* database.

2. Choose **Tools → Macro → Macros**.

3. In the list box, select the macro you want to run; (*AdmissionMacro*) then click **Run** to run the macro.

Assigning a Macro to a Button

Once you have created a macro to automate repetitive tasks, you can assign the macro to a toolbar button to make it much easier to use. This way, you don't have to remember a shortcut key combination to use it. This is extremely time effective when your macro is saved to the *Personal Macro Workbook* as opposed to *This Workbook* option. The only macros available for use in all workbooks are the macros saved to *Personal Macro Workbook*. In that wise, before you assign a macro to a toolbar button, check to see where it is saved. Otherwise, you will end up with a toolbar button that does nothing most of the time.

To assign a macro to a toolbar button, follow these steps:

1. Display the toolbar on which you want to place your macro button (this could be any toolbar—Standard or Formatting).

2. Click **Tools → Customize**

3. Click the **Commands** tab

4. Choose **Macros** from the **Categories** list.

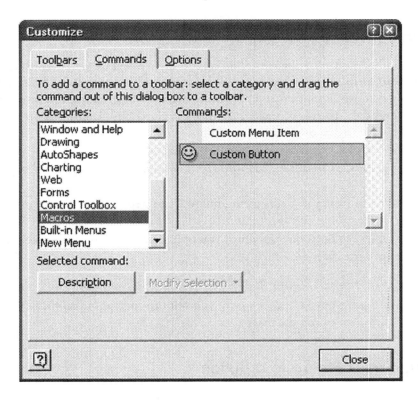

5. Select **Custom Button** under *Commands* list and drag it onto the Standard toolbar. (Remember, you have to drag the *Custom Button* to the toolbar of your choice to activate the *Modify Selection* option.)

6. Click **Modify Selection** and that should activate the following dialogue window:

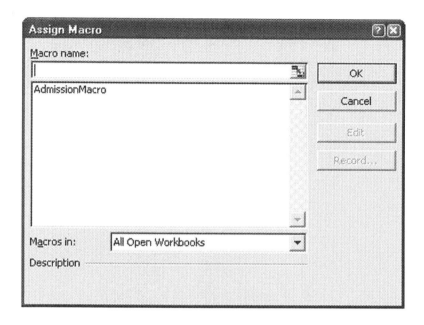

7. Click the macro name **AdmissionMacro** and click **Ok.**

> "It is the constant and determined effort that breaks down all resistance, sweeps away all obstacles."
>
> Claude M. Bristol

Chapter Nineteen

Producing Worksheet Output

Objectives

When you finish this chapter, you will be able to:

- Print Excel worksheet
- Send worksheet as e-mail attachment
- Post worksheet on the Internet
- Perform life calculations on the Internet

A mother and baby camel are talking one day when the baby camel asks, "Mom why have I got these huge three-toed feet?"

The mother replies, 'Well son, when we trek across the desert, your toes will help you to stay on top of the soft sand."

"Ok" says the son. A few minutes later, the son asks: "Mom, why have I got these great long eyelashes?"

They are there to keep the sand out of your eyes on the trips through the desert," the mother camel answered.

Thanks, Mom," replies the son. After a short while, the son returns and asks, "Mom, why have I got these great big humps on my back?"

The mother, now a little impatient with the baby camel, replies, "They are there to help us store water for our long treks across the desert so we can go without drinking for a long period of time."

"That's great, Mom. So we have huge feet to stop us sinking, and long eyelashes to keep the sand from our eyes and these humps to store water, but…Mom?"

"Yes, son? What is it this time?"

"Why the heck are we in the San Diego Zoo?"

What is the purpose of this story? Once you master all the features of Excel, and you know how to produce an excellent spreadsheet, you must be willing to show your work to its intended audience. Excel has a lot of options to help you produce output of your worksheet or make them available where they are mostly needed and useful. Some of these options include:

1. Printing your worksheet for viewing and sharing

2. Sending the worksheet as e-mail attachment

3. Making your worksheet available over the Internet

Printing your worksheet

Unlike *Microsoft Word*, Microsoft Excel provides easy access of all its print options through the Page Setup dialog box. In the Page Setup dialog box, Excel allows you to make different choices, thereby do more than adjusting the page orientation. You can set margins, headers and footers and also take advantage of other highly useful options as well. From the Page Setup, Excel will actually let you print preview your worksheet, define and control the final output before printing begins and input header and footer plus more. A snapshot of the Page Setup window is hereby presented for your convenience:

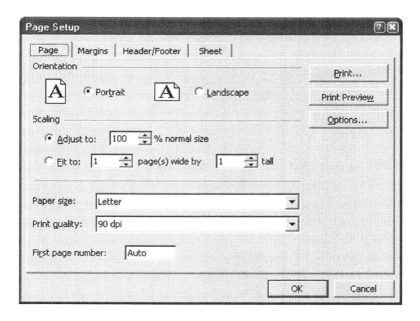

How to print Excel Worksheet with row numbers

Steps:

1. Click **File** → **Page Setup**, and then click the **Sheet** tab.

2. Under **Print**, click in the check box next to **Row and Column Headings** to select it.

3. Click **Print**.

Create Headers and Footers

A header is a piece of text (usually the title, company name or the name of the author of your worksheet) that is repeated at the top of each page. On the other hand, footer is a text that is repeated at the bottom of each page. Excel is designed to automatically produce some pre-designed headers and footers from which you can choose, or create a custom header or footer depending on your need.

1. To add a pre-designed header or footer, follow these steps:

2. Click **File → Page Setup** to open the *Page Setup* dialog window.

3. Click the **Header and Footer** tab to activate the following dialog window:

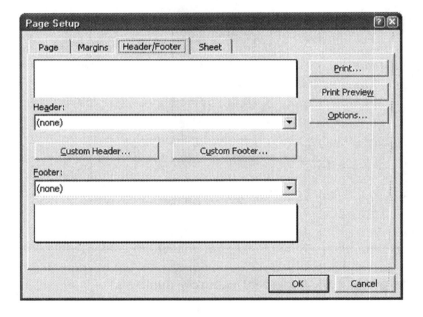

4. Click the little tinny arrow to the right of the box under **Header** (the box is currently displaying *(none)*) to pick any of the pre-designed Header from those listed.

5. Do the same to select Footer.

6. Click **Ok.**

Create a custom Header or Footer

1. Click **File → Page Setup** to open the page dialog window.

2. Click the **Header/Footer** tab

3. Click either the **Custom Header** or the **Custom Footer** to activate the following window

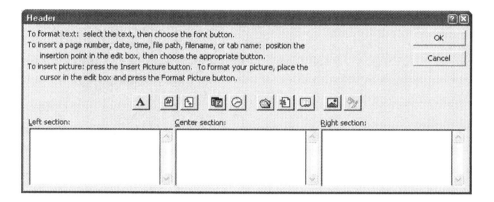

4. Click the **Left Section** to add text such as your company's name

5. Click the **Center Section** to perhaps add page number, and finally

6. Click the **Right Section** to add something like the author's name or the company's address

Notepad

If you are going to use the ampersand, (&), in the company's name, as in **Larry & Joe Limberg,** you must type the ampersand twice. This is highly necessary and required. It tells Excel that you intend to use the ampersand as part of your text and not trying to specify code syntax. In this case, you will type the company's name as **Larry && Joe Limberg** (no space between the two ampersands). Should you like to know more about the subject of Header and Footer in Excel, feel free to visit www.mednetservices.com from time to time for lots of Free downloads.

Print two worksheets from separate workbooks on the same page

Do you have data on two or even more Microsoft Excel worksheets that you'd like to print on a single page? If you had been wondering if this is really possible, wonder no more. I am happy to let you know that it is possible. You can actually produce a combined printout, even if the worksheets are in different workbooks. The first thing to do is open a new worksheet and create links to the two or more separate worksheets that you would like to print.

For example, let's assume you have Financial Statement on one worksheet, Balance Sheet on another and Changes in Financial Position on yet another worksheet.

Let's further assume that you plan to continue keeping the report (Financial Statement, Balance Sheet and Changes in Financial Position) and the details on their respective separate worksheets as it's currently the case. However, you want to print them all on the same page. Follow these steps:

1.   Open a blank worksheet. For example, you could add a sheet to the workbook and name it Financial Report.

2.   Open the Financial Statement worksheet. Click **Select All** to select the entire worksheet.

3.   From the **Edit** menu, click **Copy**.

4.   Go back to the new worksheet (the one you named Financial Report), click the upper-left cell of the area where you want the data to appear. For example, to place the Financial Statement at the top of the page, all you need to do is click cell **A1**.

5.   On the **Edit** menu, click **Paste special**, and then click **Paste Link**. This new action would link data on the new worksheet to its original source. This is necessary and required if you want changes to the original worksheet to automatically appear on the new worksheet.

6.   To format the cells on the new worksheet to match the original range of data from the data source, click **Paste special** again, and then click **Formats**.

7.   Now go to the other worksheet (the Balance Sheet worksheet) containing the next range of data that you want to print on the same page. Select the exact range of data that you want to copy.

8.   Go back to the new worksheet (the one you named Financial Report), click the cell where you want the data to appear.

9. From the **Edit** menu, click **Copy**. Do not forget to let the new area remain selected.

10. Go back to the **Edit** menu, click **Paste special**, and then click **Paste Link**. To copy the formatting too, click **Paste special** again, and then click **Formats**.

11. Repeat steps 7 through step 10 to copy Changes in Financial Position to the new worksheet.

Print Large Worksheet to fit one page

Depending on your data, you might want to adjust column widths or row heights. Formatting and adjustments affect only the new worksheet, and not the original worksheets that you're linking to.

1. When you've finished with the new worksheet and you are ready to print, click **File,** and then click the **Page Setup** to set any print options you want before you print the new worksheet. For example, if the new worksheet is too large but you would rather have it on one page anyway, do the following:

   a. Click the radio button next to **Landscape**, and also the radio button next to **Fit to** under *Scaling*.

   b. Make sure the **Fit to** be left at page **1** and the **page(s) wide by** is also left at **1**. Depending on the size of your worksheet, Microsoft Excel would let you print on Letter size paper or Legal size paper.

2. It is advisable to use the new worksheet for printing purposes, and continue to maintain your data on the original worksheets.

3. When you open the workbook containing the new worksheet (Financial Report), make sure you update links, and the new worksheet will always reflect the latest changes to the original data in the data source.

Notepad
For more information on this subject and other subjects discussed in this book, feel free to visit www.mednetservices.com from time to time for lots of Free downloads.

Using standard Print dialog window

You can always use the standard **Print** dialog window to generate a hard copy of your worksheet by doing the following:

1. Click **File → Print** and this should activate the Print dialog window

2. Under *Print Range,* click **All** to print your entire workbook or select *Page range*

3. Under *Print what,* click to print the **Active Sheet(s)** or click to print the **Entire Workbook.**

4. Under *Copies,* do not forget to indicate the **Number of copies** as well as whether you want to **Collate** while printing

5. Click **Ok** to start printing.

E-Mail Attachment—Online Collaboration

We need to be mindful of the fact that the lack of face-to-face contact places a premium on sharing information efficiently. By the same token, we need to be equally mindful of the fact that it is undoubtedly easier and faster to exchange documents and other types of information nowadays than anytime in the history of human existence—thanks to the Internet.

A Loan Amortization worksheet due to be presented to the Board of Directors this afternoon in San Diego can be prepared by a Certified Public Accountant whose office is in New York, sent to the Medical Director who is attending a symposium in Singapore (and a copy sent to the Senior Vice President who is on vacation in Lagos, Nigeria) for review and approval. The same document can be sent to the Sr. Vice President who is on her way to a business conference in Geneva, Switzerland and still be made available on time in San Diego, California.

Microsoft Excel 2000, XP and 2003 are designed to make it easier for you to send your worksheet to any recipient for review or as an attachment to an e-mail.

To send your worksheet, follow these steps:

1. When you finish preparing your worksheet, click **File → Send To.**

2. Choose **Mail Recipient (for review)**…or **Mail Recipient (as attachment)**…

3. Depending on the option of your choice, you might be asked to save your worksheet with a different name to keep track of changes made by the intending recipient.

4. The system should activate Microsoft Outlook, arrange your email with your attachment in place just like the following screen:

5. Unless you intend to add more messages, the next step should be to supply the recipient e-mail address and click **Send** button on the message toolbar to send your message.

Save e-Mail Attachment

In this section, I am going to assume that your *Microsoft Outlook Express 6* is configured to send and receive e-mail messages using your existing e-mail account. If that is the case, all you need to do to save any attachment file that comes with your e-mail message is follow these steps:

1. Click the **Send/Receive** button on the Outlook Express toolbar to download all your new e-mail messages

2. Open your **e-Mails** one by one

3. When you come across the one with attachment, click on **the attachment** and you would be presented with an option to **Save Attachment**.

4. Click on it to save the attachment to the directory of your choice.

Posting your worksheet on the Internet

Every application program in Microsoft Office 2000 and Office 2002 is designed to make integration with the Web a lot easier. You can post Microsoft Excel worksheet as an interactive Web page or non interactive Web page. Any of these would probably help to increase the usefulness of the worksheet.

Web Page Preview

To preview your worksheet in a web browser without publishing it, do the following:

1. Make sure the worksheet you intend to preview is the one currently displaying on your Microsoft Excel.

2. Click **File → Web Page Preview.**

3. If after you clicked Web Page Preview and the same Excel file is still showing, go to the Status bar and look for a file opened by your Internet Explorer, and click on it.

4. Depending on the size of your worksheet, you may have to scroll to view the entire sheet.

Publish a workbook as an interactive Web page

Follow these steps:

1. Click **File → Save** to save your workbook in regular Excel format before you publish your workbook as interactive Web Page.

2. Click **File → Save as Web Page** to activate the following *Save As* dialog window

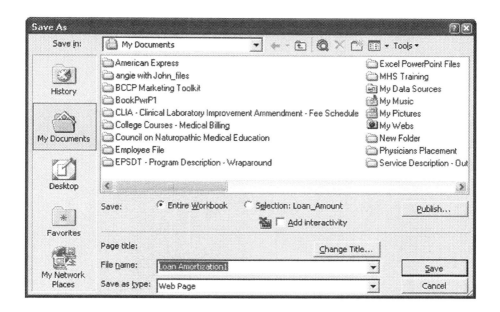

3. Click the **Save In** box to select the folder you want to publish to (this is usually a folder within your web folder).

4. Select **Entire Workbook** to publish the workbook in Web format

5. Click the check box next to **Add Interactivity.** As soon as you click this, the system would change your **File Name** to, probably a default name such as *Page.htm*. Feel free to change the name to reflect the worksheet name but do not forget to include the (**htm**) extension.

6. Click **Publish.** (This will only publish to the folder you specified in step 3 above. However, feel free to preview your interactive page in your browser before you publish your entire web page(s) to the Internet.)

> "If you find it in your heart to care for somebody else, you will have succeeded."
>
> Maya Angelou

Chapter Twenty

Protecting sensitive patient information using Microsoft Office 2003

Objectives

When you finish this chapter, you will be able to:

- Understand steps toward HIPAA compliance
- View content with restricted permission
- Create content with restricted permission
- Protect a document from unauthorized changes

Applies only to: Word, Excel and PowerPoint 2003

HIPAA is the acronym for the Health Insurance Portability and Accountability Act of 1996. The Centers for Medicare & Medicaid Services (CMS) is responsible for implementing various provisions of HIPAA.

The Administrative Simplification provisions of the Health Insurance Portability and Accountability Act of 1996 (HIPAA, Title II) require the Department of Health and Human Services to establish national standards for electronic health care transactions and national identifiers for providers, health plans, and employers. It also addresses the security and privacy of health data. Adopting these standards will improve the efficiency and effectiveness of the nation's health care system by encouraging the widespread use of electronic data interchange in health care.

Steps toward HIPAA compliance

Healthcare providers deal with sensitive patient information on daily basis—the type of information that is protected by the HIPAA law. Sensitive patient information stored electronically can only be controlled by limiting access to the networks or computers where the information is stored.

Microsoft Office 2003 offers a new feature known as the Information Rights Management (IRM). Information Rights Management helps you prevent sensitive information from getting into the hands of the wrong people, whether by accident or carelessness. IRM essentially helps you control your files even after they have left your desktop, thereby making it easier to maintain 100% compliance with HIPAA law.

IRM allows an individual author to create a document, workbook, or presentation with restricted permission for specific people who will access the content. Authors use the **Permission** dialog box—**File** → **Permission** → **Do Not Distribute** or **Permission** on the **Standard toolbar** to give users Read and Change access, as well as to set expiration dates for content. For example, Ms. Jones can give her supervisor permission to read a document but not make changes to it. Ms. Jones can then give the Medical Director permission to make changes to the document, as well as allow him to save the document. Ms. Jones may also decide to limit both her supervisor and the Medical Director's access to this document for a specified number of days. As the author or the entity in charge of sensitive information, IRM permits full control.

Implementation of HIPAA rules at all level is required. When a restricted permission is established and you later on change your mind, the restricted permission can be removed from the document, workbook, or presentation by simply clicking **Unrestricted Access** on the **Permission** submenu or by clicking **Permission** again on the **Standard** toolbar. Restricting access is expected to ensure safe delivery and not designed to keep it away from those who will need it for effective and efficient patient care.

Access levels

Users or groups can be given a set of permissions according to the access levels assigned to them by authors using the **Permission** dialog box:

1. **Read** Users with Read access can read a document, workbook, or presentation, but they don't have permission to edit, print, or copy.

2. **Change** Users with Change access can read, edit, and save changes to a document, workbook, or presentation, but they don't have permission to print.

3. **Full Control** Users with Full Control access have full authoring permissions and can do anything with the document, workbook, or presentation that an author can do: set expiration dates for content, prevent printing, and give permissions to users. Authors always have Full Control access.

Viewing content with restricted permission

Users who receive or open content with restricted permission simply need to open the document, workbook, or presentation just as they would with content that doesn't have restricted permission. In Word, Excel and PowerPoint, users can view the permissions given to them in the **My Permission** dialog window shown below:

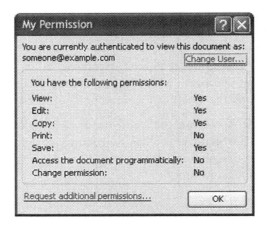

If a user does not have Office 2003 or later installed on their computer, the user can download "Rights Management Add-on for Internet Explorer" that allows them to view the restricted content. To download the Add-on, log on to this website: http://www.microsoft.com/windows/ie/downloads/addon/rmupdate.mspx

Create content with restricted permission

We are going to use the *Information Rights Management* available only in *Microsoft Office Professional Edition 2003, Microsoft Office Word 2003, Microsoft Office Excel 2003*, and *Microsoft Office PowerPoint 2003*.

1.   Start *Microsoft Office Word 2003* and open the letter created earlier.

2.   Click the **File** menu, point to **Permission**, and then click **Do Not Distribute**.

3.   In the **Permission** dialog box, select the **Restrict permission to this** *<file type>* check box.

4.   In the **Read** and **Change** boxes, type the names or e-mail addresses of people you want to give permission to.

If you want to give all users permission, click **Give all users Read access** to the right of the **Read** box, or click **Give all users Change access** to the right of the **Change** box.

5. Click **OK.** Do not forget to save your document and distribute to your designated users with permission granted above.

Set an expiration date for content

1. From the **Permission** dialog box, click **More Options**.

2. Under **Additional permissions for users**, select the **This** *<file type>* **expires on** check box, and then select an expiration date from the calendar.

Allow users to view content without *Microsoft Office 2003*

1. From the **Permission** dialog box, click **More Options**.

2. Under **Additional settings**, select the **Allow users with earlier versions of Office to read with browsers supporting Information Rights Management** check box.

Require users to connect to the Internet to open content with restricted permission

1. From the **Permission** dialog box, click **More Options**.

2. Under **Additional settings**, select the **Require a connection to verify a user's permission** check box.

Change a user's access level

1. From the **Permission** dialog box, click **More Options**.

2. In the list of users who have permission, click the user you'd like to change the access level for.

3. Under **Access Level**, point to the current access level for that user, click the arrow, and then select a new access level.

View content with restricted permission

If you want to view the permissions you have for any document with restricted permission, click the **Status** tab in the **Shared Workspace** and then click the **View my permission** link

Protect a document from unauthorized changes

To actually protect a document from unauthorized changes or use, the best approach is to seal your document with a digital signature in a digital certificate. "A digital signature (as defined by Microsoft) is an electronic, encryption-based, secure stamp of authentication on a macro or document. This signature confirms that the macro or document originated from the signer and has not been altered. If you do not already have a digital certificate, you must obtain one. You can obtain a digital certificate from a commercial certification authority, such as VeriSign, Inc., or from your internal security administrator or Information Technology (IT) professional. Or, you can create a digital certificate yourself using the Selfcert.exe tool."

How to create a Test Certificate

Microsoft Office 2000 includes a program that you can use to create digital certificates for signing Microsoft Visual Basic for Applications (VBA) projects. The program is called *SelfCert.exe*. You can use *SelfCert.exe* to create "test certificates" that you can use to sign VBA projects.

> **Warning:** A sound knowledge of program installation as well as a sound knowledge of *Microsoft Office* is required before making the attempt to create digital certificate.

"Digital signatures that are created with the *SelfCert* program are for personal use only. They are not meant for commercial distribution of VBA solutions. The type of certificate that is generated does not verify your identity."

To create a test certificate for use with your VBA projects in Microsoft Office 2000, follow these steps:

1. Click the Windows **Start** menu, point to **Programs**, and then click **Windows Explorer**.

2. If the Windows Explorer takes you to My Documents directory, click the down arrow in the address block to locate *Local Disk (C:)*. Click *Local Disk (C:)* and navigate to the *Program Files*\Microsoft Office\Office9. *Office9* is the folder where you installed Microsoft Office 2000. While in Office9, scroll down to locate *SelfCert.exe* and install it. If you are using

Microsoft Windows 2003, you can access *Windows Explorer* by doing the following: Click **Start** → **All Programs** → **Accessories** → **Windows Explorer.**

Notepad

The SelfCert.exe program is not part of the standard installation of Microsoft Office 2000. In that wise, you may have to install *SelfCert.exe* from the original *Microsoft Office 2000 CD* on your development computer system. If you need to install the *SelfCert.exe* program, rerun Setup for Office CD1 and click **Add or Remove Features.** Click the plus sign (+) next to **Office Tools**; click **Digital Signature for VBA Projects** and then click **Run from My Computer.** Click **Update Now.**

3. After *SelfCert* starts, type your name in the **Your name** box, and click **OK.**

This will generate a digital certificate for the name you supplied.

Adding a Digital Signature to a Macro Project in Office XP and Office 2003

SelfCert.exe is installed as part of Microsoft Office XP and Office 2003

1. Open the file that contains the macro project that you want to sign.

2. Click **Tools** → **Macro**, and then click **Visual Basic Editor.**

3. In the Project Explorer, select the project that you want to sign.

4. From the **Tools** menu, click **Digital Signature.**

5. Do one of the following:

    a. If you did not select a digital certificate, or if you want to use a different digital certificate, click **Choose**, select the certificate that you want, and then click **OK** twice. or

    b. Use the current certificate, and then click **OK.**

Require a password to open or modify a document

Use strong passwords that combine upper- and lowercase letters, numbers, and symbols. Example of Strong password: *B2L048N.* Example of Weak password: *Dog297.* Use a strong password that you can remember so that you don't have to write it down.

1. Open the file (the document you would like to protect with password).

2. Click the **Tools** menu, click **Options**, and then click **Security** tab.

3. From the *Security* tab, do one of the following:

   Create a password to open

   a. In the **Password to open** box, type a password, and then click **OK**.

   b. In the **Reenter password to open** box, type the password again, and then click **OK**.

   Create a password to modify

   a. In the **Password to modify** box, type a password, and then click **OK**.

   b. In the **Reenter password to modify** box, type the password again, and then click **OK**.

This concludes our coverage of Microsoft Office for Healthcare Professionals. The next edition would focus more on integration within *Microsoft Office* family of programs as well as database management. I would also look into how you can make *Microsoft Office* an integral part of your claims processing and eligibility verification.

About the Author

Dr. Henry Balogun is the Chairman & CEO of MedNet Healthcare Systems. He is an acclaimed healthcare/IT consultant—author of *Beyond Cut, Copy and Paste*. He's been teaching in Pennsylvania at the Bucks County Community College in the Nursing & Allied Health department since the fall of 2003. One of the courses he is currently teaching includes Microsoft Office for Healthcare Professionals.

Index

0-595-34353-8